Seeds of
Faith

Seeds of Faith

Randall K. Mehew

Other works by Randall K. Mehew:

- A Most Convincing Witness
- Personal Life History Outline
- Our Family History Guide
- A Precious Gift, A Novel
- Gospel Basics Busy Book, Vol. I
- Gospel Basics Busy Book, Vol. II
- The Best Manners Book Ever
- Organizing Families & Reunions
- Struggle for the Soul (Book and Cassette Tape)
- Historical Outline of the Book of Mormon

Contents

Preface

In his timeless discourse on faith, the prophet Alma taught that the true word of God can be compared to a seed. The seed, small and tender, first sprouts then begins to grow as it is properly nourished. These growing or swelling motions can be felt as the seed matures to enlarge the soul and enlighten the understanding.

Alma further taught that, although a seed of faith may be planted, each individual's responsibility is to nourish it so that the seed may take root in fertile soil and grow to its greatest potential. Hence, by constant diligence, patience, and nurturing the seed will become "a tree springing up unto everlasting life," bringing forth fruit that is most sweet and precious above all other.

In *Seeds of Faith*, latter-day prophets and church leaders share the words of counsel in this composite volume of twenty important principles and laws of the gospel of Jesus Christ. Collectively, these principles encompass nearly every facet of life. Gaining eternal life will be determined to a great degree on how well these principles, along with all principles of the gospel, are honored and incorporated into our lives. The express purpose of *Seeds of Faith* is to assist readers to more fully understand and become conversant with these basic principles of the gospel.

Introduction

*"If thou lovest me, thou shalt serve me
and keep all my commandments"* (D&C 42:29).

The essence of this guide to better living is to encourage the quiet resolve to lengthen our stride economically, intellectually, physically, and spiritually as individuals and as families so that we may be better prepared to meet the ordinary day-to-day requirements of successful living and ultimately receive eternal life and exaltation with our Heavenly Father.

One of the principal purposes of this life is to find out if the Lord *can* trust us. In one of our familiar scriptures the Lord says, ". . . we will prove them herewith, to see if they will do all things whatsoever the Lord their God shall command them." (Abr. 3:25.) We are destined to be tried, tested, and proven during our sojourn on earth to see if we are trustworthy.

The Prophet Joseph Smith indicated that to attain the highest blessing of this life, we will first be tested and proved thoroughly until the Lord is certain that he can trust us in all things, regardless of the personal hazard or sacrifice involved. The Lord loves all of his children, but he can trust some more than others. It is far better when he can both love *and* trust each one of us.

The Lord has told us, "If you will that I give unto you a place in the celestial world, you must prepare yourselves by doing the things which I have commanded you and required of you." (D&C 78:7.)

Our obedience to being fully prepared should not be based on ignorance and apathy for the programs and laws that the Lord has placed upon the earth. We must be diligent in seeking after righteousness and living the gospel, for men cannot be saved in ignorance.

The Lord has told us also that, "men should be anxiously engaged in a good cause, and do many things of their own free will, and bring to pass much righteousness;

"For the power is in them, wherein they are agents unto themselves. And inasmuch as men do good they shall in nowise lose their reward." (D&C 58:27-28.)

To the person who becomes absorbed in achieving eternal goals, life becomes more abundant. Nothing is more invigorating than working hard to fulfill a noble and worthwhile purpose.

The Prophet Joseph Smith said, "Happiness is the object and design of our existence; and will be the end thereof, if we pursue the path that leads to it; and this path is virtue, uprightness, faithfulness, holiness, and keeping all the commandments of God." (*History of the Church*, 5:134-135.)

"The place to begin is here. The time to start is now. The length of our stride need be but one step at a time. God, who has designed our happiness, will lead us along even as little children, and we will by that process approach perfection." ("Developing Spirituality," Howard W. Hunter, *Ensign*, May 1979. p. 26.)

Hartman Rector, Jr. stated in a conference address that, "When the Lord said, 'Lengthen your stride, quicken your pace, heighten your reach, widen your vision, and stretch your capacity,' he was in reality saying 'expect a miracle,' for these are the stuff from which miracles are made.

"The prophet says, 'DO IT,' and he indicates the time is NOW. And expect the miracle." (*Ensign*, May 1979, p. 31.)

Today we live in troubled times. Evil is rampant in the world. Satan is waging an all-out offensive against the work of God and against all that is good, wholesome, and uplifting. We face dangers as great as any faced by the

Lord's children anciently. Today the Lord continues to warn us through his chosen servants, the prophets.

The principles outlined in this book are fundamental basic commandments that the Lord has revealed through his prophets since the beginning of time. The Lord has said that in our day "the voice of warning shall be unto all people, by the mouths of my disciples" (D&C 1:4). To those who heed this voice of warning — listening to the words of the living prophets and keeping all the commandments — the Lord has promised great blessings, including peace in this life and eternal life hereafter.

President Spencer W. Kimball has said: "We continue to warn the people and plead with them, for we are watchmen upon the towers, and in our hands we have a trumpet which we must blow loudly and sound the alarm." (*Ensign*, Nov. 1975, p. 7.)

President Kimball also has stated:

> Some may wonder why General Authorities speak of the same things from conference to conference. . . .
>
> Prophets say the same things because we face basically the same problems. Brothers and sisters, the solutions to these problems have not changed. It would be a poor lighthouse that gave off a different signal to guide every ship entering a harbor.
>
> We shall move forward, brothers and sisters, to live a life of worthiness. We shall pay our tithes and offerings; we shall attend the temple and look after the genealogical data for our dead. . . . We shall teach our children righteousness. We shall send our sons worthily on missions. We shall attend to our own responsibilities in teaching our neighbors the gospel and warning them. (*Ensign*, May 1976, pp. 8, 108.)

The Brethren know our true potential. They keep telling us that we were sent here to succeed, that we were foreordained for the work, that we *can* do it, and that if we are true to ourselves and what we know, we *will* do it. Soon it becomes clear enough that the spotlight isn't going to move to anyone else, that we are simply going to have to come through and that no one is going to ratify the excuses we had ready to use in case we failed.

Brigham Young said:

> The Lord created you and me for the purpose of becoming Gods like Himself; when we have been proved in our present capacity and have been faithful with all things He puts into our possession. We are created, we are born for the express purpose of growing up from the low estate of manhood, to become Gods like unto our Father in heaven. This is the truth about it, just as it is. The Lord has organized mankind for the express purpose of increasing in that intelligence and truth, which is with God, until he is capable of creating worlds on worlds, and becoming Gods, even the sons of God. (*Latter-day Prophets Speak*, p. 71.)

As we ponder upon the words and teachings of the Lord through his prophets contained within this published work, seek the inspiration of the Lord for guidance and direction in the areas that you may be weak in and need strengthening. In the back of the book are goal sheets for outlining needs and solutions.

May we all remember the wisdom and direction in the following scripture as we earnestly strive for perfection:

"Trust in the Lord with all thine heart, and lean not unto thine own understanding;

"In all thy ways acknowledge him, and He shall direct thy paths." (Proverbs 3:5-6.)

The end result of our efforts in our eternal progression is summarized by Elder Joseph Anderson: ". . . if we are to have eternal life in the true sense, we must render obedience to the gospel of Jesus Christ, the plan of life and salvation which he has revealed. Only thereby can we obtain the reward of exaltation and eternal life in the presence of our Heavenly Father in his celestial kingdom.

"The reward for doing good is joy and happiness in this life and eternal life in the great hereafter." ("Being Anxiously Engaged," *Ensign,* May 1978, p. 70.)

"If you will that I give unto you a place in the celestial world, you must prepare yourselves by doing the things which I have commanded you and required of you." (D&C 78:7)

"Organize yourselves, prepare every needful thing . . ." (D&C 88:119)

"Watch therefore: for ye know not what hour your Lord doth come." (Matthew 24:42)

"But the day of the Lord will come as a thief in the night . . ." (II Peter 3:10)

"If ye are prepared, ye shall not fear." (D&C 38:30).

Sustain Church Leaders 1

☐ *Sustain local and General Authorities of the Church in prayer, and in faith; abide by their counsel in thought, word, and deed.*

> *"Thou shall give heed unto all his (the prophet's) words and commandments which he shall give unto you . . . for his words ye shall receive, as if from mine own mouth, in patience and faith".* (D&C 21:4-5).

We as members of the Church of Jesus Christ of Latter-day Saints should carefully guard against any unkind or improper words being spoken against any of the Lord's anointed servants.

"Cursed are all those that shall lift up the heel against mine anointed, saith the Lord . . ." (D&C 121:16-18).

It sometimes seems easier to sustain and support the General Authorities of the Church than those who are appointed to preside as officers, quorum leaders, bishops, or stake presidents. Can we honestly follow counsel from the authorities of the Church if we refuse or ignore directions from those whom we live among and know well? Do we reverence the man or the office to which he is called?

President John Taylor said: "I acknowledge every man in his place and office, whether president, bishop, priest, teacher or deacon; and then they should acknowledge everybody over them. . . . Do not be too anxious to be too smart, to manage and manipulate, and to put things right; but pray for those that God has placed in the different offices of this Church that they may be enabled to perform their several duties. The Lord will sustain his servants and give them his Holy Spirit and the light of revelation" (*The Gospel Kingdom*, p. 167).

Elder Boyd K. Packer has said: "The man who will not sustain the bishop of his ward and the president of his stake will not sustain the President of the Church" ("Follow the Brethren," *BYU Speeches of the Year*, Mar. 23, 1965, p. 5).

Since the time of Adam, the Lord has revealed his word to his servants, the prophets, to direct his kingdom on earth. Today is no different. The Lord Jesus Christ guides His Church on a daily basis and inspires his prophets and revelators.

The prophets are the Lord's mouthpiece on earth and our salvation depends on it. That is why we must sustain them by *praying* for them every day for the inspired guidance they need of the Lord; by *studying* their words in the Church publications; and *following* their teachings completely.

The prophet is the President of the Church and has the right to revelation for the entire Church. He holds the "keys to the kingdom". No one except the president can receive God's will for the membership of the Church.

In the 132nd section of the *Doctrine and Covenants*, the Lord declared that the prophet speaks for the Lord in everything (see vs. 7). The prophet speaks on both spiritual and temporal affairs of living which are inseparably connected as the Lord has stated: "All things unto me are spiritual, and not at any time have I given unto you a law which was temporal" (D&C 29:24).

President Wilford Woodruff made this statement: "I say to Israel, the Lord will never permit me or any other man who stands as president of the Church to lead you astray. It is not in the program. It is not in the mind of God. If I were to attempt that, the Lord would remove me out of my place, and so he will any other man who attempts to lead the children of men astray from his oracles of God and from their duty . . ." (*The Discourses of Wilford Woodruff*, Bookcraft, 1969, pp. 212-213.)

When the prophets speak about what we need to know, it is not always what we *want* to hear. The prophet is not limited by man's reasoning as what the Lord says is right, and what we say is right. We read in Isaiah 56:5-6: "For my thoughts are not your thoughts, neither are your ways my ways, saith the Lord.

"For as the heavens are higher than the earth, so are my ways higher than your ways, and my thoughts than your thoughts."

Changes and more changes will come to the kingdom of God from the Lord as it is strengthened and perfected on earth. As Latter-day Saints, we must accept change and continued inspired guidance. In April 1883, President John Taylor received a revelation from the Lord which the following is an excerpt: "Fear me and observe my laws and I will reveal unto you from time to time, through the channels which I have appointed, everything that shall be necessary for the future development and perfection of my Church, for the adjustment and rolling forth of my kingdom, and for the building up and the establishment of my Zion" (James R. Clark, comp., *Messages of the First Presidency*, 2:354).

President Taylor also spoke of the need for continuous revelation in the management of the Church: "We require . . . living intelligence, proceeding from the living priesthood in heaven, through the living priesthood on earth. . . ." (*The Gospel Kingdom*, p. 34).

Before becoming the President of the Church, Harold B.

Lee explained how the Church would be guided: "I am sure that by the time we arrive at the place where we need more revelations that the Lord will give that light and knowledge to the prophet whom he has put upon the earth for that purpose" (*Improvement Era*, Jan. 1962, p. 36). Later, as a member of the First Presidency, he added: "Nobody changes the principles and doctrines of the Church except the Lord, by revelation. But *methods* change as the inspired direction comes to those who preside at a given time . . . the fundamental doctrines of the Church are *not* changing. The only changes are in the methods of teaching that doctrine to meet the circumstances of our time" (*Ensign*, Jan. 1971, p. 9, italics added).

Summarizing the words of wisdom and counsel by President Ezra Taft Benson on following the prophet of the Lord, he said:

> The words of the living prophets take precedence to the words of the dead prophets. . . . The words of the living prophets are more important to us today for *our* salvation than the words of the Standard Works. . . . The Quorum of the First Presidency is the highest council in the Church, follow them. . . . The prophet does not have to say, 'Thus saith the Lord' to be scripture. . . . The honest in heart will heed his words while the wicked men of the world and the learned and rich who are proud will mentally stone him. . . . Follow the prophet and be blessed, if not, suffer. (see BYU Devotional, Feb. 26, 1980, see 2 Ne. 9:28-30).

At the solemn assembly in which President Spencer W. Kimball was sustained as prophet, seer, and revelator, he said:

> . . . We are grateful, deeply grateful for your sustaining vote. Our only interest now is to advise and counsel the people aright and in total line with the counsels of the Lord as they have come through the generations and

dispensations. We love you people and wish for you total progress and joy and happiness, which we know can come only through following the admonitions of God as proclaimed through his prophets and leaders" (*Ensign*, May 1974, p. 46).

Family Unity/
Honor Parents
2

☐   *Marry in the temple; seal the family; have concern for spouse and children; raise children up in righteousness; honor parents.*

> *"No other success can compensate for failure in the home. Unity, harmony, and goodwill are virtues to be fostered and cherished to make a home a bit of heaven on earth."* — David O. McKay (*Conference Report,* Oct. 1967 p.7)

Real families are not created simply through the birth of children. Strong family ties do not happen by chance. Family unity is forged by time, patience, service, and sacrifice.

President Gordon B. Hinckley has said: "Our Father in Heaven, who loves his children, desires for them that which will bring them happiness now and in the eternities to come, and there is no greater happiness than is found in the most meaningful of all human relationships — the companionships of husband and wife and parents and children" (*Ensign,* May 1974, p. 23).

President Brigham Young has told us that our families are not yet ours. The Lord has committed them to us to see how we will treat them. Only if we are faithful will they be given to us forever.

Our family can be together forever. To enjoy this blessing we must be married in the temple, performed by one who holds the sealing powers and authority. The temple of the Lord is the only place this holy ordinance can be performed.

The Lord has said: "If a man marry a wife by . . . the new and everlasting covenant . . . by him who is anointed . . . it . . . shall be of full force when they are out of the world" (D&C 132:19).

An eternal marriage is ordained of God and that is how he wants it for all his children. An eternal marriage gives us the opportunity to continue as families after this life, but we are reminded by the Lord that these blessings depend upon our obedience and faithfulness to the laws of God. Nothing can part us forever except by our willful disobedience. This is why it is important to work harder to have a successful and happy marriage.

The goal of every Latter-day Saint should be the goal of eternal marriage. President Spencer W. Kimball has taught that "marriage is perhaps the most vital of all the decisions and has the most far-reaching effects. . . . We recommend . . . that all boys and girls from their infancy up plan to be married only in the temple . . . to keep their lives spotless so that this can be accomplished" (". . . The Matter of Marriage," Devotional address, Salt Lake Institute of Religion, Oct. 22, 1976).

Every child born to Latter-day Saint parents deserves to be born "under the covenant" of temple blessings. Elder O. Leslie Stone has said: ". . . To you who were married for time only, let me urge you to thoroughly investigate the blessings available to you by going to the temple and having your family sealed to you for time and all eternity. Participating in these sacred ordinances should be your most important objective for achieving a successful marriage" (Ensign, May 1978, p. 56).

Our exaltation depends on marriage. Our Heavenly Father has given us the law of eternal marriage so that we can become like him. We must live the law of eternal marriage to become like he is—able to have spirit children. The Lord has said: "In the celestial glory there are three heavens or degrees; And in order to obtain the highest, a man must enter into this order of the priesthood (meaning the new and everlasting covenant of marriage); And if he does not, he cannot obtain it." (D&C 131:1-3).

In this regard, President Joseph Fielding Smith wrote:

> No man shall receive the fulness of eternity, of exaltation alone; no woman shall receive that blessing alone; but man and wife, when they receive the sealing power in the temple of the Lord, if they thereafter keep all the commandments, shall pass on to exaltation, and shall continue and become like the Lord. And that is the destiny of men; that is what the Lord desires for his children (*Doctrines of Salvation*, 2:44).

The Lord said that if we lived this principle of exaltation, "Ye shall come forth in the first resurrection; . . . and shall inherit thrones, kingdoms, principalities, and powers. . .; (Ye) shall pass by the angels, and the gods, . . . to (your) exaltation . . ., which glory shall be a fulness and a continuation of the seeds forever and ever. Then shall they be gods, . . ." (D&C 132:19-20)

Elder O. Leslie Stone in his remarks about making marriage successful said, "It is important to reach an understanding on what is expected of each of the marriage partners. One of the first things a couple must do is establish and maintain good relations with each other. Demonstrate consideration at all times for each other. By your actions let everyone know you love each other" (*Ensign*, May 1979, pp. 56-57).

President Spencer W. Kimball, in counseling husbands and fathers concerning courtesy to their wives and family members, said: "I like to think of providing for our own as including providing them with affectional security as well as economic security . . . our obligation (is) to maintain loving affection and to provide consideration and thoughtfulness as well as food" ("Fundamental Principles to Ponder and Live", *Ensign*, Nov. 1978, p. 43).

"As husbands and wives we should be thoughtful and kind to each other. We should never do or say anything to hurt the feelings of the other. We should also try to do everything possible to make each other happy" (Milton R. Hunter, *Conference Report*, Oct. 1971, p. 50).

Home responsibilities and rearing children must be uppermost in the minds and actions of parents if a successful marriage is to be achieved. President Harold B. Lee taught: "The most important of the Lord's work that you will ever do will be the work you do within the walls of your own home. . . ." (*Decisions for Successful Living*, pp. 248-49).

Parents should teach their children the gospel. The Lord has said in the 68th section of the *Doctrine and Covenants:* "Inasmuch as parents have children in Zion, or in any of her stakes which are organized, that teach them not to understand the doctrine of repentance, faith in Christ the Son of the living God, and of baptism and the gift of the Holy Ghost by the laying on of hands, when eight years old, the sin be upon the heads of the parents" (vs. 25).

"The Lord holds parents accountable for training their children in righteousness. . . .

"We cannot evade the responsibility. Only by properly planning and charting our family life can we guide our children and keep them free from the pitfalls that lead to sin and destruction, and put them on the pathway to happiness and exaltation" (Spencer W. Kimball, *The Miracle of Forgiveness*, p. 258).

President David O. McKay has said:

> When one puts business or pleasure above his home, he, that moment, starts on the downgrade to soul-weakness.

When the club becomes more attractive to any man than his home, it is time for him to confess in bitter shame that he has failed to measure up to the supreme opportunity of his life and flunked in the final test of true manhood. . . . The poorest shack in which love prevails over a united family is of greater value to God and future humanity than any other riches. In such a home God can work miracles and will work miracles. (*Conference Report*, Apr. 1964, p. 5)

Parents are stewards over some of Heavenly Father's children. Parents have the responsibility to teach them the principles of the gospel and lead them in righteousness. Consider the counsel of Elder A. Theodore Tuttle concerning the priorities of parenthood:

This decision to be parents means to put *first*, the obligation to be baby-sitters, trainers, discipliners, supervisors, teachers, assigners, checker-uppers, planners, storytellers, exemplars, and, in short, to be common, ordinary, garden variety, old-fashioned, on-the-job, full-time parents. It means that this responsibility as parents comes before social climbing, . . . It supersedes personal selfishness, propriety, pleasure, even a tidy house. It demands solemn and continual allegiance to a cause greater than self. Fulfillment of this parental duty develops all of the virtues that can be named, . . . this privilege, as the Lord had intended, requires a *conscious decision* to accept the responsibilities of this sacred obligation — the most sacred and far-reaching obligation assumed by two people. ("And They Shall Also Teach Their Children," *Relief Society Magazine*, 50:484-85, July 1963)

It is possible for families to be united in temporal things such as camping, sports, hobbies, or family traditions. These activities are commendable, but they are incomplete, however, unless balanced by spiritual goals as well. Family togetherness alone is not sufficient. Family efforts are to be directed toward both eternal goals and appropriate temporal concerns.

There is no better chance for children to develop spiritually than to have loving parents who pray together, counsel frequently about the spiritual needs of their children, and take the vital teaching steps necessary to meet those needs.

The greatest of all teaching methods parents can use is the example of their own lives. We should teach our children that we are what we say. Of this, Elder Marion D. Hanks testified: "Young people learn more from our conduct as parents and adults than they do from the lessons we deliberately undertake to teach them. They acquire the quality of integrity not so much from pronouncements as from observing and associating with people in whom integrity is the established norm" (*Ensign,* Nov. 1975, p. 25).

> Fatherhood is leadership, the most important kind of leadership. It has always been so; it always will be so. Father, with the assistance and counsel and encouragement of your eternal companion, you preside in the home. It is not a matter of whether you are most worthy or best qualified, but it is a matter of law and appointment. . . . It is your place to give direction relating to all of family life.
>
> You give father's blessings. You take an active part in establishing family rules and discipline. As a leader in your home you plan and sacrifice to achieve the blessing of a unified and happy family. To do all of this requires that you live a family-centered life (*"Father, Consider Your Ways"* pamphlet, p. 4-5).

A child leaving to go away to school or on a mission, a wife suffering stress, a family member being married or desiring guidance in making an important decision — all these are situations in which the father, in exercise of his patriarchal responsibility, can bless his family.

The home should be a place where reliance on the Lord is a matter of common experience, not reserved for special occasions. One way of establishing that is by regular, earnest prayer. It is not enough just to pray. It is essential that we really speak to the Lord, having faith that he will reveal to us what we need to know and do for the welfare of our families.

Satan knows how important families are to our Heavenly Father's plan. He has set out to destroy them by keeping us from drawing near to the Lord and having His spirit with us. Satan will tempt us to do things that will draw our families apart.

All of us want to have happy, successful families. The following points are ways to achieve that goal:

1. Improve family prayers in such a way as to increase unity in the family and hold them night and morning.

2. Set the goal to hold weekly family home evenings and make them more meaningful opportunities for teaching gospel principles.

3. Have daily family scripture study time.

4. Attend Church meetings regularly together as a family unit.

5. Plan work projects and outings together as a family.

6. Set aside a time to be alone with a child, where undivided attention is given. Spending time with that child doing what he or she enjoys the most or maybe just *making* occasion to be together. This is a good opportunity to teach gospel principles when in private conversation.

Other suggestions to strengthen family ties are:

1. Listen carefully and long to the children with an open heart, and try to understand what they are saying. Encourage each child to share his innermost feelings and problems about school, friends, and church. President

Spencer W. Kimball has asked: "Fathers, are you so busy making a living, playing golf, bowling, hunting, that you do not have time to talk to your boys and hold them close to you and win their confidence? Or do you brush them off, so that they dare not come and talk . . . with you?" (*The Miracle of Forgiveness*, p. 258). This advice would also extend to mothers with daughters.

Elder A. Theodore Tuttle has said: "Fathers, draw close to your children. Learn to communicate. Learn to listen. This means giving a father's most valuable commodity — time! Only good results occur when a father interviews his sons and daughters regularly. He can know their problems and their hopes . . . we become friends with our children in unconditional love, to the extent we become like our Heavenly Father" (*Ensign*, Jan. 1974, p. 67).

2. Look for the good traits in the children. Praise and acknowledge accomplishments and the things they do right.

3. Use restraint when chastising children; discipline with love and patience (see D&C 121:43-44).

4. Parents, support and honor each other in front of the children.

5. Set just family rules and consistently follow them.

6. Teach correct principles as soon as children are ready to assimilate them and by allowing the children the freedom to apply them. This love and training for their welfare cannot be postponed. It must start early in life.

7. Meet the challenge of the media. The key to the intelligent use of the media in the home is the teaching of discernment and development of discriminating tastes.

8. Provide opportunity to be responsible. Children need opportunities to work at home and elsewhere, getting plenty of practice in making decisions and following through on commitments, and being responsible for their own repentance.

9. Enthrone love and respect for each other. Parents must lead the way by encouraging, praising, respecting and warmly accepting and guiding children.

10. Study the children and their world. Understand why children act as they do, and keep abreast of changes in their world.

11. Set goals and evaluate progress as parents and as a family in family councils on a regular basis.

Children share with their parents the responsibility of building a happy home. In commanding children to honor their parents, the Lord has said: "Honor thy father and thy mother, that thy days may be long upon the land" (Exodus 20:12). To honor parents means to love and respect them and their wisdom. It also means to obey them. The scriptures tell children to "obey your parents in the Lord: for this is right" (Ephesians 6:1).

Can a father expect to draw the hearts of his children to himself if his own heart is not drawn out to bless, help, and care for his own parents? Can a priesthood holder expect the power of heaven to seal his wife and children to him if he does not do all in his power to honor his parents?

President Spencer W. Kimball has said that Church members "should take care of their fathers and mothers, no matter if they do become senile, no matter if they do become difficult to handle. They should be taken care of; that is part of the program of the Lord" (*Ensign*, Nov. 1976, p. 127).

A father and mother, with their children, counseling together, should make whatever adjustments and sacrifices necessary so that aging parents may be properly and lovingly cared for.

"We can learn to respect the wisdom, experience, and value of older people. . . . With careful planning, a family can have loving, rewarding experiences in caring for its elderly members. There is no better way to teach children respect for the elderly and the need for everyone to prepare for that time in life than by helping to care for their older relatives." (Barbara B. Smith, "In Time of Old Age", *Ensign*, May 1978, p. 85).

President Spencer W. Kimball has said: "If we truly honor our parents as we are commanded to do, we will seek to emulate their best characteristics and to fulfill their highest aspirations for us. Nothing we could give them materially would be more prized than our righteous living." (*Ensign*, May 1978, p. 101).

In summary, President Kimball further states his concerns about family unity:

> As local Church leaders cautiously conserve the time that families can spend together, we say to both parents and children, "Come back home" . . . Young men and women must balance their involvement in school and other social activities with supportive participation in family activities and appropriate time in the home.
>
> All should work together to make home a place where we love to be, a place of listening and learning, a place where each member can find mutual love, support, appreciation, and encouragement ("Living the Gospel in the Home", *Ensign*, May 1978, p. 101).

Elder James M. Paramore has also challenged us to a commitment to our families:

> We affirm that every life is sacred and important. Every child is a gift and a blessing. The home is an institution of learning, of loving — to develop the capacities of each of its members to live in accordance to the laws of God. We testify that these laws are eternal and unchanging. A personal commitment to this priority is paramount. Nothing can surpass the inner security of having one's family committed to God. . . .

Prophets in all ages have counseled families to pray, study, work, and play together, to bind ourselves together in all holiness. It is and ever will be the answer to happiness, peace, and unity in this world. But it takes a commitment to do so — to do all we can. Knowing is not enough! It takes a personal commitment to be 'anxiously engaged,' to do *everything* possible ("A Personal Commitment", *Ensign*, May 1979, p. 61).

Personal & Family Prayer   3

☐ *Have meaningful daily personal and family prayers.*

"The basic exercises of the Spirit—prayer, reverence, worship, devotion, respect for the Holy—need to be actively practiced in our lives" —Howard W. Hunter (*Ensign,* Nov. 77, p. 52).

Prayer is a sincere, heartfelt talk with our Heavenly Father through our mediator and Elder Brother, Jesus Christ. The commandment to call upon God in the name of the Son has never been taken away.

The Prophet Joseph Smith stated, "It is the first principle of the gospel to know for a certainty the Character of God, and to know that we may converse with him as one man converses with another." (*Teachings of the Prophet Joseph Smith,* p. 345.)

"Men and women of integrity, character, and purpose have ever recognized a power higher than themselves and have sought through prayer to be guided by that power. Such has it ever been. So shall it ever be.

". . . There is no expiration date on the Lord's injunction to pray. As we remember Him, He will remember us." (Thomas S. Monson, "The Prayer of Faith," *Ensign,* May 1978, p. 20-21).

Our Heavenly Father is always near. Whatever we do or wherever we are, we are never alone. We can reach out and receive His aid and tap that unseen power through prayer, without which no man can do his best.

Our thoughts, our words and actions are influenced by our prayers. We should pray frequently, at least two or three times each day, "morning, midday and evening" as the Prophet Alma in the Book of Mormon (See Alma 34:21) and our present day Church leaders have counseled. We can pray whenever we feel the need to communicate with our Heavenly Father, whether silently or vocally. At times we need to be alone, without distractions, where we can pour out our souls to our Heavenly Father about our hopes, our desires, and our needs.

If we don't feel like praying, then we should prepare and humble ourselves for prayer. "Prayer is the pulsation of a yearning, loving heart in tune with the Infinite. It is a message of the soul sent directly to a loving Father. The language is not mere words but spirit vibration." (*Treasures of Life*, p. 308).

The great Prophet Moroni counseled us that we should always pray in faith, "with a sincere heart, with real intent. . . ." (Moroni 10:4).

Elder Howard W. Hunter has stated:

If prayer is only a spasmodic cry at the time of crisis, then it is utterly selfish and we come to think of God as a repairman of a service agency to help us only in our emergencies. We should remember the Most High, day and night, always — not only at times when all other assistance has failed and we desperately need help. If there is any element in human life on which we have a record of miraculous success and inestimable worth to the human soul, it is prayerful reverential, devout communication with our Heavenly Father. ("Hallowed Be Thy Name," *Ensign*, Nov. 1977, p. 52).

The first and eighth verses of the favorite hymn, *Prayer Is the Soul's Sincere Desire* read:

Prayer is the soul's sincere desire,
Uttered or unexpressed,
The motion of a hidden fire
That trembles in the breast.

Oh thou by whom we come to God,
The Life, the Truth, the Way!
The path of prayer thyself hast trod;
Lord, teach us how to pray. (Hymns, No. 220).

President Ezra Taft Benson has said:

Our prayers should be meaningful and pertinent. We should not use the same phrases at each prayer. Each of us would become disturbed if a friend said the same few words to us each day, treated the conversation as a chore, and could hardly wait to finish it in order to turn on the TV and forget us.

In all our prayers it is well to use the sacred pronouns of the scriptures — Thee, Thou, Thy, and Thine — when addressing Deity in prayer, instead of the more common pronouns of you, your, and yours. In this arrangement we show greater respect to Diety ("Prayer", *Ensign,* May 1977, p. 33).

In praying, we should *first thank our Father in heaven for our welfare* and the comfort he gives us daily. Above all, we should give our *expressions of love* to He who gave us life itself and for the blessings we receive. We should also ask for *strength to resist temptation* of Satan and his followers and to *help us overcome our problems.* We need to ask for the *Lord's guidance and help in our daily affairs,* and *confess our sins and shortcomings and ask forgiveness.* We should *pray for protection against our enemies* and in *giving us direction in living* the gospel more fully; also for the *inspiration and well being of our Church and government leaders*, our family members, neighbors, and friends. At the end of our prayers, we should *close in the name of Jesus Christ*, our mediator between us and the Father.

The Lord has also commanded us and given us the privilege to kneel together and have family prayers so that our families may be blessed (see 3 Ne. 18:21). We have been counseled by our Church leaders to pray as families each morning and evening taking turns as family members in offering thanks for his blessings and asking for those things the family needs.

In asking of the Lord for his blessings, we should ask that *His* will be done. After making a request through prayer, we have a responsibility to assist in its being granted. We need to remain on our knees and *listen*. Sometimes the Lord wants to counsel us through the 'still small voice'.

Our Heavenly Father always answers our sincere prayers. Sometimes the answer may be no. That which we desire may not be the best for us. (See Ne. 18:20) Sometimes the answer is yes, and we have a warm, comfortable feeling about what we should do (see D&C 9:8-9). Sometimes the answer is "wait awhile". Our prayers are always answered at the time and in a way that the Lord knows will help us the most.

Often God gives us the power to help answer our own prayers. As we pray for help, we should be doing all we can to bring about the things we desire.

Two important scriptures come to mind concerning prayer: *"Be thou humble; and the Lord thy God shall lead thee by the hand, and give thee answer to thy prayers."* *(D&C 112:10.)* *"Trust in the Lord with all thine heart, and lean not unto thine own understanding. In all thy ways acknowledge him, and he shall direct thy paths." (Proverbs 3:5-6).*

If we follow the example of the Prophet Enos in the Book of Mormon (see Enos 1-5) we can increase the power of prayer in our lives through sincere daily communication which draws us nearer to our Heavenly Father.

Let us often remember these words: "Man never stands taller than when upon his knees."

Family Home Evening/ Family Councils   4

☐ *Hold weekly Family Home Evenings on gospel subjects; hold Family Councils regularly.*

> *"We stress the family home evening in every home every week, that we may be able to guide and inspire and train and give leadership to the thoughts toward spiritual growth and religious inspiration"*
> — Spencer W. Kimball (*Ensign*, May 1976, p. 107.)

The educational testimony set forth in the opening lines of the *Book of Mormon* is challenging and instructive:

"I, Nephi, having been born of goodly parents, *therefore I was taught* somewhat in all the learning of my father . . ." (I Ne. 1:1; italics added).

Within the gospel of Jesus Christ, the Family Home Evening Program is committed to the belief that the family is the most important institution in all the world. We must give preference in time and energy to the family and observe properly and conveniently the family home evening. The First Presidency has given a promise to the Saints concerning family home evening:

"If the saints obey this counsel, we promise that great blessings will result. Love at home and obedience to parents will increase. Faith will be developed in the hearts of the youth of Israel, and they will gain power to combat the evil influences and temptations which beset them"

(Spencer W. Kimball, N. Eldon Tanner, Marion G. Romney).

Home and family *are* the most important, the most influencial institutions of Society, educationally as well as religiously. Less problems will arise within the home if love and respect are taught, practiced, and nurtured there.

The Lord instituted the Family Home Evening Program as a basis for religious instruction in the home. Moses' prophetic instructions in Deuteronomy concerning the teaching of children in the home is enlightening:

"Thou shalt love the Love thy God with all thine heart, and with all thy soul, and with all they might.

"And these words, which I commanded thee this day, shall be in thine heart:

"And thou shalt teach them diligently unto thy children, and shalt talk of them when thou sittest in thine house, and when thou walkest by the way." (Deut. 6:5-7.)

President Kimball has stated:

Regarding our home evenings, an evening home with the family or an evening out to some place of interest with your family only partly solves the need of the home evening. Basically important is the teaching of the children the way of life that is vitally important. Merely going to a show or a party together, or fishing, only half satisfies the real need, but to stay home and teach the children the gospel, the scriptures, and love for each other and love for their parents is most important. (*Ensign,* Nov. 1977, p. 4).

In another conference address, President Spencer W. Kimball also remarked:

Since the home is the basis for the nation, we move forward to see that our children are taught and trained and controlled, since they are the most precious possession we have; and we teach them to walk uprightly and to become worthy citizens of the kingdom of God.

We recognize the fact that the teaching of religion and morality certainly is the work of the parents of the children. It is the responsibility of the fathers and mothers.

That is why we stress the family home evening in every home every week, that we may be able to guide and inspire and train and give leadership to the thoughts toward spiritual growth and religious inspiration. (*Ensign*, May 1976, p. 107.)

Concerning the teaching of children, Elder G. Homer Durham has explained:

What shall we teach our children? The Lord has outlined the basic curriculum found in the *Doctrine and Covenants*, Section 68 versus 25-30: First, teach the *doctrine of repentance*. To some the word may sound ominous, but none need shrink from it. It is the road to progress. The most glorious opportunities for true joy and happiness are found in this doctrine.

Second, teach *faith in Christ the Son of the living God*. Children taught to have faith in him can follow his example in doing good to all. Such will serve well their fellow beings. . . .

Third, teach *baptism and the gift of the Holy Spirit by the laying on of hands, when eight years old*. This provides entrance to the Church itself, a large family circle. The gift of the Holy Ghost follows as the means of leading us into all truth. . . .

Fourth, to make such teaching effective, the Lord has said in this same section: *Parents shall also teach their children to pray, and to walk uprightly before the Lord.* (D&C 68:28.)

Fifth and finally, *diligent, intelligent industry* must be taught as the key to all this and to all achievement. All inhabitants of Zion are counseled in this section "to labor in all faithfulness" (D&C 68:30). Work habits are best taught at home. ("The Home as an Educational Institution," *Ensign*, May 1979, pp. 10-11).

A royal family is a family whose members are honest, true, chaste, benevolent, virtuous, temperate, patient, charitable, humble, diligent, well read, and law-abiding. The Lord has cautioned, "But I have commanded you to bring up your children in light and truth" (D&C 93:40).

If fathers and mothers will gather their family together once each week and discuss the gospel principles with the many instructional materials provided by the Church and other well-meaning resource materials and learn the gospel, then they are magnifying their callings as parents. For "inasmuch as parents have children in Zion, or in any of her stakes which are organized, that teach them *not* to understand . . . the sin be upon the heads of the parents." (D&C 68:25; italics added).

By learning the gospel through an organized plan within the framework of a regularly held family home evening program, families will have a more meaningful relationship in their lives as a unified family. A well-planned calendar with gospel purposes for a three-month period will make the program more meaningful and the Lord will pour out his blessings ten-fold.

Family home evenings need not be elaborate or formally conducted. Minutes should be kept and assignments made involving everyone with a responsibility. Simplified lessons or discussions are more effective if everyone in the family can participate and add to its success. If a quiet reverence exists, the spirit of the Lord will be present. Activities with the family are encouraged but should be held at another time other than the religious, instructional period of the home evening.

The home is the basic unit of the Lord's kingdom here on the earth. His house is a house of order. If family problems arise in the home or needs need to be discussed, a Family Council should be held where all members of the family may participate by discussing the facts and offering solutions, directed towards both eternal goals and temporal concerns and then voting on them in a systematically and orderly way.

Holding family councils regularly perfects the family organization. Throughout these procedures, we are teaching one another divine principles of God's government. By doing so, we are following the admonition of the Lord: "Organize yourselves, prepare every needful thing." (D&C 88:119.)

May we follow the admonition of President Spencer W. Kimball: "Let us move forward with clear vision and sound judgment, and rededicate our homes and our families to high moral and spiritual values." (*Ensign*, May 1976, p. 107).

Scriptural Study 5

☐ *Read and study the scriptures daily both individually and as a family.*

"Search the scriptures; for in them ye think ye have eternal life: and they are they which testify of me." (John 5:39)

Scripture is the Lord's counsel to man on earth, through his servants, the prophets. We should study the scriptures every day, for in them we will find peace and knowledge of pure truth of the nature of God and his plan of salvation. The answers to every problem we may encounter on this earth are found in the scriptures.

If we desire to avoid the evils of the world and the buffetings of Satan, we must feed our minds with the truth and righteousness found within the scriptures. We will never grow closer to God than by reading and pondering his words.

Joseph Smith has told us that the Book of Mormon is "the most correct of any book on the earth, and the keystone of our religion and a man would get nearer to God by abiding by its precepts, than by any other book" (*History of the Church*, 4:461).

The Church of Jesus Christ on the earth today accepts four Standard Works as the word of God and scripture: *The Bible,* which includes the Old and New Testament, the *Book of Mormon,* the *Doctrine and Covenants,* and the *Pearl of Great Price.*

In the *Articles of Faith* by Joseph Smith, which scripture is found within the Pearl of Great Price, it states: "We believe all that God has revealed, all that he does now reveal, and we believe that he will yet reveal many great and important things pertaining to the Kingdom of God." (Ninth Article).

The inspired words of our living prophets become scripture to us today, as did the prophets of old who spoke in ancient times. We receive their words of inspiration and revelation through general conferences and other public addresses, Church publications and by other instructional means. When the Lord's servants speak or write under the influence of the Holy Ghost, their words become scripture (see D&C 68:4). That is why we have been encouraged to subscribe to the Church magazines: the *Ensign* for the adult membership of the Church; *The New Era* for the youth; and *The Friend* for the children.

From the beginning of the earth since Father Adam, the Lord has commanded his prophets to keep a record of his revelations and his dealings with his children, ". . . for out of the books which shall be written I will judge the world, every man according to their works, according to that which is written" (2 Ne. 29:11).

In order for us to be able to gain eternal life and exaltation we must search the scriptures and glean the knowledge necessary to properly live those principles outlined therein by the Lord.

Elder LeGrande Richards has given us food for thought concerning the value of the holy scriptures:

If we didn't have the holy scriptures, what would we know about our Father in heaven and his great love that gave us his Only Begotten Son? What would we know about his Son and his great atoning sacrifice, and the gospel that he has given us, the pattern of life to live by, and the principles . . . of where we came from, why we are here, and where we are going? ("Value of the Holy Scriptures," *Ensign*, May 1976, p. 82).

By reading the scriptures we gain a greater knowledge of three fundamental concepts in God's eternal plan:

1. The divinity of Jesus Christ, the Son of God.
2. The divine mission of the Prophet Joseph Smith, the head of this, the last dispensation of the earth.
3. The divine mission of the Church of Jesus Christ in these latter days.

The scriptures should be shared with the children where they will learn to love them and use them for the truths the scriptures contain. Scriptural reading together as families will foster greater concern for each other and nurture love and understanding between family members. That is the purpose of the word of the Lord to his children.

President Spencer W. Kimball has emphasized that, "No father, no son, no mother, no daughter should get so busy that he or she does not have time to study the scriptures and the words of modern prophets" (*Ensign*, May 1976, p. 47).

Each Latter-day Saint should undertake a consistent program of serious scripture study. It has been proved by many that the entire Standard Works of the Church can be read in one year if fifteen (15) minutes a day is consistently used for scripture reading.

A system of marking and recording passages should be

developed and then reviewed on a weekly basis and evaluation of progress made each month. Pick a time each day that will best suit daily schedules, and then stick to it every day! Some individuals prefer reading the scriptures in the early morning to help start the day off right. Others like to read at lunchtime for a spiritual midday boost. Others prefer evening reading and study to end the day's activities. Whatever time is used, use it consistently, never letting a day pass by without reading.

Prayer should begin the study period by asking the Lord for inspiration and a clear mind. After reading and studying, ponder for a few moments the scriptures that were read. Pray again for understanding of what was read and think of ways in which it may be beneficial in this life of progression.

The Holy Ghost will bear witness to us of the truth of that which we read in the scriptures. Moroni bore testimony of that witness, saying: ". . . and if ye shall ask with a sincere heart, with real intent, having faith in Christ, he will manifest the truth of it unto you, by the power of the Holy Ghost.

"And by the power of the Holy Ghost ye may know the truth of all things" (Moroni 10:4-5).

Sabbath Day Observance 6

☐ *Observe fully the Sabbath day and give reverence to the Lord.*

". . . thou shalt go to the house of prayer and offer up thy sacraments upon my holy day; For verily this is a day appointed unto you to rest from your labors, and to pay thy devotions unto the Most High" (D&C 59:9-10)

The word *Sabbath* comes from the Hebrew word meaning, *day of rest.* From Adam's time the Lord has revealed that one day in seven is to be a holy day, a day which he has blessed and made sacred. It is a day of joy when we rest from all the burdens, worries, and work of the week and come close to Him. The seventh day in the week was consecrated by the Lord as a Sabbath.

We need the Sabbath! Because the Lord loves us, he gave us laws to obey which would bring us happiness and eternal life with Him. But he knew that we would not keep these laws unless we kept them in our minds and hearts. The Lord knew that this would not be easy, so in His careful planning for us He commanded us by law to set aside one day in seven.

Jesus Christ taught that the Sabbath Day was made to benefit man (see Mark 2:27). As we rest from our usual daily activities, our minds are freed to ponder on spiritual matters and to do the Lord's work.

Pres. Ezra Taft Benson has summarized the purposes and values of the Sabbath day in these words: "The purpose of the Sabbath is for spiritual uplift, for a renewal of our covenants, for worship, for rest, for prayer. It is for the purpose of feeding the spirit, that we may keep ourselves unspotted from the world by obeying God's command" (God, Family, Country, pp. 103-104).

In a revelation given to Joseph Smith in 1831, the Lord commanded the Saints to sanctify the Sabbath day: "And that thou mayest more fully keep thyself unspotted from the world, thou shalt go to the house of prayer and offer up thy sacraments upon my holy day;

"For verily this is a day appointed unto you to rest from your labors, and to pay thy devotions unto the Most High" (D&C 59:9-10).

Keeping the law of the Sabbath means more than attending our meetings. During the sacrament our minds are focused on the Lord Jesus Christ. We must refrain from doing anything that would mar the spirit from attending us or those around us.

The Savior wants us to remember his great atoning sacrifice and to keep his commandments. To help us do so, he has commanded us to meet often and partake of the sacrament. We do it in remembrance of his flesh and blood which were given as a sacrifice for us.

As we partake of the sacrament, we renew sacred covenants with the Lord. We take upon ourselves His name, that we are identified with Him and his Church and that we will not bring shame or reproach upon that name. We covenant to remember Jesus Christ and to keep his commandments.

Worthy partakers of the sacrament put themselves in perfect harmony with the Savior. Before partaking of the sacrament, we must prepare ourselves spiritually, for the Lord has made it clear that no one should partake of the sacrament unworthily (D&C 46:4). During the sacrament service we should dismiss from our minds all worldly thoughts and feel prayerful and reverent.

The Lord promises that if we keep our covenants, we will always have his Spirit to be with us. If we partake of the sacrament with a pure heart, we will receive the promised blessings of eternal life.

The Sabbath is not a day merely to rest from work and do nothing. The Sabbath calls for constructive thoughts and acts. President Spencer W. Kimball has given an overview of some of these worthwhile observances:

> The Sabbath . . . is a day of consistent attendance at meetings for the worship of the Lord, drinking at the fountain of knowledge and instruction, enjoying the family, and finding uplift in music and song.
>
> It is a day for reading the scriptures, visiting the sick, visiting relatives and friends, doing home teaching, working on genealogy records, taking a nap, writing letters to missionaries and servicemen or relatives, preparation for the following week's church lessons, games with the small children, fasting for a purpose, writing devotional poetry, and other worthwhile activities of great variety." (*Faith Precedes the Miracle*, pp. 270-271).

Other worthwhile and uplifting activities could be: writing personal and family histories; visiting the elderly or shut-ins; reading good books and the words of Church leaders; visiting quietly with the family and getting better acquainted; personal interviews and father's blessings; preparing simple meals for the day in the right spirit with the bulk of preparation made on Saturday; and prayers of thankfulness and gratitude to the Lord.

In deciding what activities we should properly engage in on the Sabbath, we should ask ourselves the question, 'Will it uplift and inspire me?' President Benson gives some examples of the types of activities that are *not* in harmony with the spirit on the Sabbath:

1. Overworking and staying up late Saturday, resulting in exhaustion on Sunday.
2. Filling the Sabbath so full of extra meetings that there is no time for prayer, meditation, family fellowship, and counseling.
3. Doing gardening and odd jobs around the house.
4. Taking trips to canyons and resorts, amusement centers, joy riding, loafing, etc.
5. Children playing vigorously and seeing picture shows.
6. Sports, golf, fishing, and hunting 'wild animals', . . .
7. Shopping or supporting with our patronage Sunday business — grocery stores, supermarkets, restaurants, gas stations, etc." (*God, Family, Country,* p. 105).

In summary, Sunday activities should bring us closer to the Lord. They should serve to renew our faith and refocus our attention to the Lord.

The worldliness of the present day brings more serious temptation to both young people and parents than ever before. How do we remain unspotted from the world and protect our families? The Lord has given us the answer by telling us to sincerely observe the Sabbath Day.

The First Presidency in 1928 spoke about blessings that come to families who observe the Sabbath:

> We earnestly appeal to the people to keep their meeting appointments faithfully and to utilize that portion of Sunday not appointed for meetings in promoting family association in the home, with the purpose of stimulating and establishing greater home fealty, a closer companionship among parents and children, and more intimate relations among all kindred.

We believe that it is unnecessary for families to go beyond their own homes or those of their kindred for the relaxation and association which are proper for the Sabbath day, and we therefore discourage more traveling than is necessary for this purpose and attendance upon appointed meetings.

Let all unnecessary labor be suspended and let no encouragement be given by the attendance of members of the Church at places of amusement and recreation on the Sabbath day. If Sunday is spent in our meetings and in our homes greater blessings will come to our families and communities (Heber J. Grant, Anthony W. Ivins, and Charles W. Nibley, *Messages of the First Presidency*, 5:260).

The prophets have been repeating those same words spoken of in 1928, and in our present day, a prophet of the Lord has warned us about the increasing lack of observance of the Sabbath throughout the world:

I again would urge upon all Saints everywhere a more strict observance of the Sabbath day. The Lord's holy day is fast losing its sacred significance throughout the world, at least our world. More and more, man destroys the Sabbath's sacred purposes in pursuit of wealth, pleasure, recreation, and the worship of false and material gods. We continue to urge all Saints and God-fearing people everywhere to observe the Sabbath Day and keep it holy. Businesses will not open on the Sabbath if they are not patronized on that holy day. The same is true of resorts, sporting events, and recreation areas of all kinds. Pursuit of the almighty dollar is winning, it seems, over the Lord's commandment, 'Keep my sabbaths, and reverence my sanctuary' (Lev. 19:30).

'Why call ye me, Lord, Lord, and do *not* the things which I say?' (Luke 6:46; emphasis added.) (Spencer W. Kimball, "Hold Fast to the Iron Rod," *Ensign*, Nov. 1978, p. 5).

Families should be taught to honor the Sabbath in such a way that children will learn to love a sacred Sabbath and believe in honoring it. This is done by constant example and sound parental counsel.

When considering ways to improve Sabbath observance, ask the question, 'How can I best instill in my family the proper attitudes and spirit about the Sabbath?' As you examine your ideas and feelings, consider the following suggestions found in the 1974 Melchizedek Priesthood study guide:

> Rather than providing your family with a list of 'do's and don'ts,' you will find that the most effective way to instill proper Sabbath observance in your home is by your personal example and proper motive. Smaller children, of course, must be positively directed to activities that are in keeping with the Sabbath day. As your children observe what you do and your motive for doing it, they will be instilled with right and holy principles or its opposite. (p. 185.)

Through proper observance of the Sabbath in a righteous manner we may receive great spiritual and temporal blessings. We can be grateful to the Lord for the gift of the Sabbath day, and by keeping it holy we will have the protection of the Lord against the evils of the world and our home and family will be fortified. The Lord has promised us that the fulness of the earth is ours and that our joy will be full if we will but keep the Sabbath holy (see D&C 53:13-19). We must analyze our own attitudes and see if we are keeping the laws so as to merit the blessings promised us.

☐ *Organize a formal immediate and grandparent family organization.*

> "There is nothing more important for a priesthood holder to do than to give consideration to the fact that he is establishing his patriarchal order here in mortal life, and that that order will be extended into the eternities." —Pres. Ezra Taft Benson (*Family Organization and Records*, pamphlet, No. PXCT0777.)

What organization is more important than wards, quorums, the Sunday School, Relief Society, Primary — and is the most important unit in the Church? It is the family, the patriarchal organized family. These other units serve it, and they make it supremely more effective in doing the Lord's work, but only the family is the eternal unit.

President Joseph F. Smith said: "Family organization lies at the basis of all true government, and too much stress cannot be placed upon the importance of the government in the family being as perfect as possible" (*Gospel Doctrine*, p. 162). On whom does the responsibility lie for family organization? In another statement, President Smith declared: "In the home the presiding authority is always vested in the father, and in all home affairs and family matters there is no other authority paramount" (*Gospel Doctrine*, p. 287).

The organization of the immediate family ordinarily includes the father, the mother, and their children who are living at home. Where there is no father in the home, the mother presides.

The Lord's counsel to fathers that they should set in order their families, represents a great opportunity and obligation. Blessings await families who apply the *principle* of family organization, for family organization is a principle, not a program.

Strong families are basic to building the kingdom of God. A family organization helps families to be productive in this role. Church members have been encouraged to organize on three levels:

1. *Immediate families* (with family home evening as its' basis).

2. *Grandparent families* (the father and mother; their children, whether married or single; and any grand-children).

3. *Ancestral families* (descendants of a deceased direct ancestor), wherever possible.

There are no rules we have to follow when getting organized. The Church has no definite format for family organizations. Families are just too different to all have the same kind of family organization. Some families are few in number; some have no relatives in the Church; others have been members for generations and have formed large ancestral family organizations consisting of thousands of descendants of a common ancestor.

But the size of the organization doesn't matter. It's the love, the fun, the sense of identity and of belonging that really count. It's the meeting of family needs and to stimulate appreciation for each other that's important.

"All members should . . . participate in a family organization," President Spencer W. Kimball has declared.

(*Ensign,* May 1978, p. 4.) And underlining the fact that family organizations can give us a sense of who we are — a feeling of belonging — he has further said: "It is important for us . . . to cultivate in our own family a sense that we belong together eternally, that whatever changes outside our home, there are fundamental aspects of our relationship which will never change. We ought to encourage our children to know their relatives. We need to talk of them, make effort to correspond with them, visit them, join family organizations, etc." (*Ensign,* Nov. 1974, p. 112).

Family organizations can help children to appreciate family heritage and relationships. Writing regularly or visiting grandparents, attending reunions, or preparing reports on grandparents or other ancestors in family home evening are ways to maintain close family ties.

Organizing the family for specific purposes can help bring success to the family's projects. A well-organized budget, a well-planned calendar, and cooperation and coordination involving each family member in some phase of family responsibility can help us lead our families effectively. Father, being the head of the household is the president of the family organization; mother, being the special assistant, counselor or secretary; and the children, if old enough, members of the board of directors.

Organizing the living family not only is to meet the needs of a day-to-day existence, but also to accomplish *all* the goals associated with the family's proper place in the kingdom of God. The following list summarizes some of the purposes for family organization, as patterned after the purposes of our Heavenly Father's Kingdom:

1. *Temporal Welfare* (home production and storage; financial stability, etc.)
2. *Social, intellectual, and recreational activity.*
3. *Spiritual growth.*

4. *Missionary work.*
5. *Genealogy and temple work.*

Although frequently thought of as Church responsibilities, these purposes are often best fulfilled by family members accepting offices designated in the organization to carry out the above responsibilities as needed in the family.

Activities seem to go better when they are planned and well organized than when they are not. A family that is organized and works together under priesthood direction may achieve the highest goals to which families can aspire.

The family can be strengthened and become more fully organized by:

1. Giving greater attention to home evenings and other family meetings to enable the family to study the gospel.
2. Holding family prayer more consistently.
3. Making specific assignments for chores around the home.
4. More diligently attending Church meetings and duties.
5. Taking time each day to study the scriptures together.
6. Meeting privately with individual family members; to counsel and advise, inquire about needs, and to draw closer to them through warm and sincere interviews.
7. Increasing the contribution to missionary work by fellowshipping nonmembers.

The family must be put in its proper perspective as an eternal kingdom patterned after the kingdom of God. The righteous priesthood bearer, as the family patriarch, should seek for his family the same goals which God seeks for his children (see Moses 1:39). Three significant ways in which the family can pattern itself after the kingdom of God are:

1. *Seek the blessings of the temple* for all family members, living and dead. That is the primary purpose of the family organization; to unite family members, both living and dead, in a deeper understanding of love and brotherhood in preparation for exaltation as a *complete* family unit in the Celestial Kingdom of God.

2. *Preserve records and writings* that will be meaningful and remind family members (present and future) of those things that are essential to their salvation.

3. *Establish and maintain an appropriate organization* to administer to the needs of family members. Each family unit which obeys the Gospel in its fullest, shall remain intact through all eternity and will be linked to the generation which went before until all shall be joined in one grand family.

Therefore, if we are to be worthy to live as families throughout eternity, we must develop, here and now, a family consciousness of learning to live and love cooperatively together with a feeling of brotherhood. It is in a family life that we should learn to love most deeply, sacrifice most completely, share with each other most often, and develop the greatest amount of charity.

(Note: For additional information on this subject, obtain a copy of the resource guide *Organizing Families & Reunions* by Randall K. Mehew, Keepsake Paperbacks.)

Genealogy & Temple Work 8

☐ *Qualify for a temple recommend; submit names for ordinance work regularly; perform temple work; and maintain personal and family histories.*

> *"The greatest responsibility we have in this work is to identify our ancestors and go to the temple in their behalf."* — Joseph Smith, Jr. (*Teachings of the Prophet Joseph Smith*, p. 337.)

Priesthood genealogy is, by its very nature, a family labor. Through our participation in it, the way may be opened for eternal blessings to flow into the lives of both the living and the deceased members of our family.

The Lord and his prophets have not been apologetic about giving this work to us. The Prophet Joseph Smith, in his epistle to the saints in the 128th section of the *Doctrine and Covenants*, stated: ". . . let me assure you that these are principles in relation to the dead and the living that cannot be lightly passed over, as pertaining to our salvation. For their salvation is necessary and essential to our salvation, as Paul says concerning the fathers — that they without us cannot be made perfect — neither can we without our dead be made perfect" (vs. 15).

Another modern-day prophet, President Joseph Fielding Smith, speaking of the importance of doing this work, wrote in *Seeking After Your Dead*, page 35, as follows:

> It matters not what else we may have been called to do, or what position we occupy, or how faithfully in other ways we have labored in the Church, *none are exempt from the great obligation of performance of temple work for the dead.*
>
> It is required of the apostle as well as of the humblest elder. . . .
>
> Some may feel that if they pay their tithing, attend to their regular meetings . . . perchance spend one or two years preaching in the world, that they are absolved from further duty.
>
> But the greatest and grandest duty of all is to labor for the dead. We may and should do all these other things, for which reward will be given, but if we neglect the weightier privilege and commandment, notwithstanding all our other good works, we shall find ourselves under severe condemnation.

There is a great work to do in behalf of our dead ancestors as President Spencer W. Kimball has stated: "I feel the same sense of urgency about temple work for the dead as I do about the missionary work for the living, since they are basically one and the same . . ." (Conference Address, *Ensign,* May 1978, p. 4).

On April 3, 1836, when the Prophet Elijah was sent by the Lord to the earth and appeared to the Prophet Joseph Smith in the Kirtland Temple, he committed to the earth the sealing powers and the keys of "turning the hearts of the fathers to the children and the children to the fathers", a fulfillment of prophesy (see Malachi 4:5-6; D&C 111:13-16).

Since that day in 1836, genealogy research throughout the world has accelerated rapidly. It is by this same spirit of Elijah in the hearts of men that has caused millions to seek after their ancestral forebearers so that the saving ordinances might be performed in behalf of their dead in the temples of the Lord.

Researching our genealogy, submitting names, and attending the temple to perform the ordinances pertaining to salvation and exaltation are the three steps in doing temple work for the dead:

1. *Researching our genealogy:* We cannot do temple work for our dead ancestors unless we know who our progenitors are. Genealogy research is the vital step in identifying those who have died, so that we can not only perform baptisms for them, but likewise the higher ordinances including the sealing of their immediate families as we have ours sealed here. This important data includes their given name, place of birth, date of birth and the names of their parents. The Family History Department of the Church at 50 E. North Temple, Salt Lake City, Utah 84150 can give much assistance in research.

As members of the Church, our responsibility is to gather records and information about our ancestors for four generations. With recent developments in computer technology and communications, it now seems possible to handle the large volume of work that will be required in order to perform ordinances for the billions who have passed away. Using these resources, the Church will help us, but we must do our part by providing, through the Four Generation Program and other efforts, the names of our ancestors organized and ready for temple ordinance work. *This is our responsibility!* For that reason we should be determined to complete our four generation research and be prepared to assist in other ways.

President Ezra Taft Benson has instructed the saints: "We want to emphasize again and place squarely upon the shoulders of . . . individuals and their families the obligation to complete the four-generation program . . ." (*Ensign,* Nov. 1978, p. 30).

The four-generation program includes information on

ourselves, our parents, our grandparents, and our great grandparents on both sides of the family. This would total eight Family Group Records Sheets. A Pedigree Chart should also be completed to show the four generation organization.

Accuracy is to be emphasized. These records are part of a Church-wide effort to compile and perfect all the generations of Adam. Therefore, information on these records must be checked and rechecked to ensure accuracy.

The Lord's mandate given in section 128 of the *Doctrine and Covenants* has not changed as the Prophet Joseph Smith records: "Let us, therefore, as a Church and a people, and as Latter-day Saints offer unto the Lord an offering in righteousness; and let us present in his holy temple . . . a book containing the records of our dead, which shall be worthy of all acceptation" (vs. 24).

The standards of accuracy in genealogy can be assured by following these basic steps:

    A. Get proper documentation.
    B. Be thorough but reasonable.
    C. Be consistent but logical.
    D. Proofread for accuracy.

2. *Submitting names:* When family group records of ancestry are completed, we should then submit them for temple ordinances to be performed for those ancestors. Only one copy for each ancestral family in the four-generation set of family group records should be sent to the Ancestral File in the Church Family History Department by the family organization representative rather than from individual family members.

These accurately submitted records will then become the basis for the computer program that will show a lineage-linked picture of ourselves and our ancestors.

(Note: For information on researching and in submitting names, obtain the booklet *Come Unto Christ Through Temple Ordinances and Covenants* from Church Distribution, No. PBGS153A.)

3. *Attending the temple for ordinance work:* Eternal blessings for the family can be obtained only in the temples of the Lord. This work applies as much to living family members as it does to the deceased and should begin with us as individuals first. We must make sure all living family members have this opportunity and then perform the ordinances in behalf of deceased ancestors.

It is the will of the Lord to bless and exalt his children. The Lord has ordained that in holy places his Saints may be endowed with power and receive covenants and ordinanaces. He has also ordained that if his Saints observe and obey all that may be required in those ordinances, they may one day become as the Lord himself and receive the fulness of eternal life.

The ordinances and covenants we make with our Heavenly Father in his holy house are necessary for our salvation and the salvation of those who have passed beyond the veil. With one exception such ordinances involve covenants of exaltation. These ordinances include: anointings, endowments, and sealings. The only exception is baptism for the dead, which is an ordinance of salvation. Some ordinances are so sacred that they can only be performed within the temples dedicated for those purposes.

Whenever the fullness of the Gospel has been upon the earth the Lord has delegated to His agents on earth the power to bind on earth and in heaven (See D&C 132:46-49). When the Holy Ghost ratifies in the heavens what man performs on earth it is said to be "sealed by the Holy Spirit of Promise (D&C 132-7). That is to say, the Holy Ghost seals or binds eternally a performance made by proper authority in the temples on the earth.

The ordinance of the endowment serves as an excellent example of how the Lord uses ordinances to reveal mysteries of godliness, that is, teach about God and his ways, as well as to give power to those who participate in the ordinance. "To endow is to provide or furnish, as with some gift, faculty or quality" (*American College Dictionary*).

In 1912 the Church published a book, *The House of the Lord*, by James E. Talmage. On pages 99-101 therein the author said of the endowment ordinance:

> The temple endowment, as administered in modern temples, comprises instructions relating to the significance and sequence of past dispensations, and the importance of the present as the greatest and grandest era in human history. This course of instruction includes . . . the absolute and indispensable conditions of personal purity and devotion to the right in present life, and strict compliance with gospel requirements. . . .
>
> The ordinances of the endowment embody certain obligations on the part of the individual, such as covenant and promise to observe the law of strict virtue and chastity, to be charitable, benevolent, tolerant, and pure; to devote both talent and material means to the spreading of truth and the uplifting of the race; to maintain devotion to the cause of truth; and to seek in every way to contribute to the great preparation that the earth may be made ready to receive her King, the Lord Jesus. With the taking of each covenant and the assuming of each obligation, a blessing is pronounced, contingent upon the faithful observance of the condition.

President Brigham Young testified of the grand purpose of the endowment for all of God's children:

> Your endowment is, to receive all those ordinances in the house of the Lord, which are necessary for you, after you have departed this life, to enable you to walk back to the presence of the Father, passing the angels who stand as

sentinels, being enabled to give them the key words, the signs and tokens, pertaining to the holy Priesthood, and gain eternal exaltation in spite of earth and hell (*Discourses of Brigham Young*, p. 416).

"Let us go to and attend to our ordinances, then when we go to the spirit world and meet with father, mother, brother or sister they cannot rise up and accuse us of negligence. . . . These (temple) ordinances have been revealed to us; we understand them, and unless we attend to them we shall fall under condemnation" (Wilford Woodruff, in *Journal of Discourses*, 13:327).

By returning often to the temple to do the ordinances for the dead, we renew our covenants with the Lord each time. Satan knows the importance of the work and will try to keep us from going to the temple. We should follow the counsel from President Spencer W. Kimball:

> There is an urgency to engage more fully in the redeeming of our kindred dead through more frequent temple attendance. All those who possess temple recommends should use them as often as possible to engage in baptisms, endowments, and sealings for the dead. Other members of the Church should concern themselves seriously with preparations to qualify for temple recommends that they, too, might enjoy these eternal blessings and also act as saviors on Mount Zion. There is an ever-increasing burden of temple work to be done by the Saints, and we should rise to meet this challenge ("Hold Fast to the Iron Rod", *Ensign*, Nov. 1978, pp. 4-5).

The temple is a sanctuary from the world. It is a bit of heaven on earth. It is a place where the blessings of eternity may rest upon those who prayerfully and obediently prepare themselves to have the companionship of the Holy Spirit. We should go to the temple worthily and continue to attend often to seek the blessings for ourselves, our families, and our ancestors that the Lord promises his children.

In addition to genealogy research and temple work for the dead, one of the things we can do to unite our families is to keep a personal record of our own lives. This record is a personal book of remembrance. Since the time of Adam, the Lord has commanded us to keep a book of remembrance (see Moses 6:8).

On the importance of record keeping, Elder John A. Widtsoe, an apostle of the Lord, once stated:

> As I view it, in every family a record should be kept of the immediate family: the father, the grandfather, the great-grandfather — at least of those of whom we have a memory. . . . It should be a book known and used in the family circle; and when the child reaches maturity and gets out to make another household, one of the first things that the young couple should take along should be the records of their families, to be extended by them as life goes on. . . . There is a strength, an inspiration, and a joy in having such a record near at hand, to be used frequently, the story of our ancestors. . . . (*Ensign*, Aug. 1976, p. 23.)

From Father Adam, records have been kept of testimonies, experiences, ordinances, blessings, histories and genealogical information connected with the family. Have we ever given thought what would it be like not to have those priceless records? Every family member should compile a Book of Remembrance which should contain family genealogies and pedigree charts of direct ancestors; ancestor sketches and photos; personal certificates; blessings; and personal histories with an emphasis on spirituality such as: cherished family and personal experiences, faith promoting experiences, and principles of the Gospel affected in one's life.

Much of the information for personal and family histories can be supplied from valuable family papers and historical possessions such as letters, diaries, news clippings, old books, pictures, documents and family heirlooms. We should be diligent in preserving our personal records, our certificates, diplomas, photographs, and other documents in preparing a life history.

Our church leaders have instructed and encouraged us to keep journals and update personal histories. "We urge every person in the Church to keep a diary or a journal from youth up, all through his life" (Spencer W. Kimball *Conference Report*, Oct. 1977, p. 4).

A personal journal should include memorable spiritual experiences or events, goals for the future, areas for personal improvements, and personal thoughts and feelings.

"People often use the excuse that their lives are uneventful and nobody would be interested in what they have done. But I promise you that if you will keep your journals and records they will indeed be a source of great inspiration to your families, to your children, your grandchildren, and others, on through generations" (Spencer W. Kimball, "Hold Fast to the Iron Rod", *Ensign*, Nov. 1978, p. 4).

President Kimball has also said: "Get a notebook. . . . Begin today and write in it your goings and comings, your deepest thoughts, your achievements and your failures, your associations and your triumphs, your impressions and your testimonies" ("The Angels May Quote From It," *New Era*, Oct. 1975, p. 5).

A personal history becomes a family treasure that enables children to emulate the virtues and personal characteristics of their forebearers. If we keep a personal record, our children and grandchildren can gain strength from our lives. This record will turn our hearts and thoughts toward our children. Then, when our descendants read our record, their minds and hearts will be turned toward us.

(Note: There are two resource guides that can be of help in writing and maintaining a personal and family history: *Personal Life History* and *Our Family History* by Randall K. Mehew, Keepsake Paperbacks.)

Missionary Work/ Fellowshipping 9

☐ *Friendship non-members; give referrals; be worthy to serve a full-time mission; as parents, prepare sons to serve; support missionary work financially.*

"No person who has been converted to the gospel should shrink his responsibility to teach the truth to others. This is our privilege. This is our duty. This is a command from the Lord" —President Spencer W. Kimball (*Ensign*, Oct. 1977, p. 3).

The Lord has declared that all people must repent and be baptized (see D&C 18:41-42). Therefore, the goal of missionary work is to increase the number of convert baptisms. The Lord and his servants have also said that the responsibility to do missionary work rests with every member of the Church:

> And again, I say unto you. I give unto you a commandment, that every man, both elder, priest, teacher, and also member, go to with his might, with the labor of his hands, to prepare and accomplish the things which I have commanded.
>
> And let your preaching be the warning voice, every man to his neighbor, in mildness and in meekness. (D&C 38:40-41).

It is evident here that the Lord expects *every* man to lift up his voice and preach the gospel of Jesus Christ in mildness and meekness.

The Lord's church has always been a missionary church. When we are converted to the gospel of Jesus Christ, one of our first desires should be to share the gospel with others, especially our own family and close friends.

We have often heard the phrase by President David O. McKay that "every member a missionary". We can also say, "every member a good neighbor". Many people are converted to friends before they are converted to principles.

President George Albert Smith testified: "The gospel of Jesus Christ . . . is a gospel of love and kindness. It will cause us, if we are living as we should, to love our neighbors as ourselves, and go out of our way, if possible, to help them understand better the purpose of life" (*Conference Report,* Oct. 1948, pp. 167-168).

There are many good people in the world, men and women "who are only kept from the truth because they know not where to find it" (see D&C 123:12). Some of these people may be our own relatives, friends or neighbors. If we are willing to share with them in a spirit of love and kindness, it will enrich our own lives and make us happier.

The Lord has told us: "It becometh every man who hath been warned to warn his neighbor" (D&C 88:81). We have been told by the prophets that we should show our neighbors that we love them before we warn them. They need to experience our friendship and fellowship.

Example is the best teacher. We can show our friends and others the joy we experience from living the gospel. The Lord said in his sermon on the mount, "Ye are the salt of the earth. . . . Ye are the light of the world . . . Let your light so shine before men, that they may see your good works, and glorify your Father which is in heaven" (Matthew 5:13-16).

As Latter-day Saints, we are to be a model of righteousness by living the commandments and become "an example of the believers" (See I Timothy 4:12). Concerning our non-member contacts, President Spencer W. Kimball has said:

Our goal should be to identify as soon as possible which of our Father's children are spiritually prepared to proceed all the way to baptism into the kingdom. One of the best ways to find out is to expose your friends, relatives, neighbors, and acquaintances to the full-time missionaries as soon as possible. Don't wait for long fellowshipping nor for the precise, perfect moment. . . . If they won't listen and their hearts are hardened with skepticism or negative comments, they are not ready. In this case, keep loving them and fellowshipping them and wait for the next opportunity to find out if they are ready. You will not lose their friendship. They will still respect you (*Ensign*, Oct. 1977, p. 6).

There are many ways to share the gospel. Consider these suggestions:

President Kimball has suggested a simple three-step approach for introducing the gospel to others: "Father you are to take the lead. With your family, *prayerfully* select one or two fine families to friendship. Decide who of all your relatives or friends you will introduce to the Church. Then, as a family, contact them. Perhaps you could plan a family home evening with them on a night other than Monday, or get together with them in any of a number of ways. Then, when these families show interest, arrange through your ward or branch mission leader to invite them and the missionaries into your home to share the message of the Restoration. If you will follow this simple procedure, you will bring a number of fine families into the Church." (cited by Gene R. Cook, *Ensign*, May 1976, p. 104).

What a great blessing to a child to grow up in a home where the family is praying for the family they are fellowshipping, when at least once each month, the family does something to let the other family know that they love them; and they too see the other family come into the Church and share the joys of the gospel.

Elder Gene R. Cook of the Quorum of the Seventy has offered these challenges concerning member missionary work:

> Stand up for the truth wherever you are, at all times, and in all places. . . . As the Lord has said, it should be done with boldness but not overbearance. . . . Feel free, when prompted, my brothers and sisters, to bear your testimony of those princples that you know to be true. Sincere feelings conveyed from heart to heart by means of testimony convert people to the truth where weak wishy-washy argumentative statements will not . . . set aside your fear, and to take strength in the Lord, and to bear your witness to the world of the truthfulness of this gospel . . . there is a real urgency, a real urgency, my brothers and sisters, for us as members of the Church to lift our warning voice to all the inhabitants of the earth ("Are You a Member Missionary?", *Ensign*, May 1976, p. 103-104).

The Lord promises us blessings for doing missionary work. He has said: "If it so be that you should labor all your days in crying repentance unto this people, and bring, save it be one soul unto me, how great shall be your joy with him in the kingdom of my Father! . . . If your joy will be great with one soul that you have brought unto me into the kingdom of my Father, how great will be your joy if you should bring many souls unto me!" (D&C 18:15-16).

The Lord has also told us that, "Ye are blessed, for the testimony which ye have borne is recorded in heaven for the angels to look upon; and they rejoice over you" (D&C 62:3).

Many saints might not have the opportunity to serve a full-time mission for the Church, but the following are other ways to sustain the missionary efforts of the Church:

1. Each member of the family can contribute regularly to the General Missionary Fund of the Church which provides financial assistance to those missionaries who live in countries outside the United States and Canada.
2. Share copies of the Book of Mormon with non-member families with a written testimony placed inside of the truthfulness of the book or share subscriptions to the Church publications.
3. Fast and pray that the doors (both of nations and the hearts of men) will be opened to the missionary work of the Lord.
4. Support and encourage stake and full-time missionaries by being referral-conscious and provide them names of interested non-members.
5. Write uplifting and encouraging letters regularly to a missionary or serviceman, bearing testimony and continue writing even if the recipient's schedule does not permit an answer.

Full-time missionaries are given the responsibility to preach the gospel to all people, to baptize them, and to teach them to do all things which the Lord has commanded (see Matthew 28:19-20).

It is said that one would never have a greater calling in this life other than that of a General Authority than by serving as a full-time missionary for the Lord Jesus Christ. The prophet has asked that *every* worthy and able young man fulfill a mission for the Lord. It is *not a choice to be made here on earth* whether or not a young man goes on a mission. The choice has already been made in the pre-existance when he was foreordained there to receive the

Holy Priesthood of God. It is not only a right, but a stewardship given.

It is the family's responsibility, not the Church's, to prepare young men for missions. Parents have the responsibility to prepare their sons spiritually, financially, and physically from the time of their birth so that they may be prepared and worthy to go on a mission. The following are suggestions in this preparation process:

Spiritual:
1. Familiarization of scriptures in the four standard works of the gospel through regular personal and family scripture study.
2. Frequent personal interviews between father and sons.
3. Gospel discussions in regularly held family home evenings.
4. Prepare and give talks.
5. Participation in compassionate and welfare service projects.
6. Regular participation in seminary and 'Church meetings.
7. Regular family fellowshipping of non-members.

Financial:
1. To the prospective missionary: Establish a savings account and add to it regularly *each* month.
2. To the parents: Establish an investment or special savings fund early in son's life.
3. Take advantage of sales on items needed for a mission.

Physical:
1. Develop and maintain an exercise program.
2. Learn how to iron clothing, cook, and techniques of cleaning.

3. Maintain cleanliness and orderliness in living. Develop good grooming habits for "you act like you look."

Obedience, organization, and discipline are the three attributes of a successful missionary. These qualities should be developed early in a young man's life. President Thomas S. Monson, a great missionary for the Lord, has stated to young men:

> You who hold the Aaronic Priesthood and honor it have been reserved for this special period in history. The harvest is truly great. Let there be no mistake about it; the opportunity of a lifetime is yours. The blessings of eternity await you. How might you best respond? May I suggest you cultivate three virtues, namely — 1) *A desire to serve.* Remember the qualifying statement of the Master, 'Behold, the Lord requireth the heart and a willing mind' (D&C 64:34) . . . 2) *The patience to prepare.* Preparation for a mission is not a spur-of-the-moment matter. It began before you can remember . . . 3) *A willingness to labor.* Missionary work is difficult. It will tax your energies. It will strain your capacity. It will demand your best effort — frequently, a second effort. Remember, the race goeth 'not to the swift, nor the battle to the strong' (Eccl. 9:11) — but to him who endures to the end ("The Army of the Lord," Ensign, May 1979, pp.35-37).

The Prophet Joseph Smith revealed these words from the Lord:

> Our missionaries are going forth to different nations, . . . the Standard of Truth has been erected; no unhallowed hand can stop the work from progressing; persecutions may rage, mobs may combine, armies may assemble, calumny may defame, but the truth of God will go forth boldly, nobly and independent, till it has penetrated every continent, visited every clime, swept every

country, and sounded in every ear, till the purposes of God shall be accomplished, and the Great Jehovah shall say the work is done (*History of the Church*, 4:540).

The restored gospel brings peace, happiness, growth and development into the lives of those who accept it and live according to its' teachings. Let us increase our effectiveness in missionary work in order that the kingdom of God may go forth at an accelerated rate, so that the kingdom of heaven may come.

Law of the Fast/ Welfare Services 10

□ *Fast 2 meals; give generous fast-offerings; extend service to others.*

> *"I would that ye should impart of your substance to the poor, every man according to that which he hath; such as feeding the hungry, clothing the naked, visiting the sick and administering to their relief, both spiritually and temporally, according to their wants"* (Mosiah 4:26).

One of the most important laws of the gospel is the fast. It is essential that each Latter-day Saint have a clear understanding of this basic law to be able to live it and obtain the blessings of God.

Fasting means to go without food and drink. Fasting is good for our bodies; it clears our minds and strengthens the body and the Spirit (see *Principles of the Gospel*, p. 175.) The law of the fast includes restraining from eating any food or drinking any water or other liquids for a period of twenty-four hours. The fast day in the Church has been designated as the first Sabbath of the month and usually begins Saturday evening after meal time and ends with the beginning of the Sabbath evening meal. It is important that we go to fast meeting on Sunday, fasting, and break the fast sometime after this meeting. Partaking of the sacrament does not break the fast.

"The Biblical fast was from sundown to sundown. This fast of twenty-four hours is entirely satisfactory unto the Lord, but the First Presidency of his Church has instructed all members that they should at least abstain from eating two meals on the first Sunday of each month. This requirement may be kept by the weakest of the saints. . . . The practice of abstaining from food, at least for two meals on the fast day . . . should be regarded as a religious duty" (Charles W. Nibley, cited in Charles A. Callis, *Fast Day and Fast Offerings*, pp. 1-2).

President Joseph F. Smith has said:

> The Lord has instituted the fast on a reasonable and intelligent basis, and none of his works are vain or unwise. . . . Many are subject to weakness, others are delicate in health, and others have nursing babies; of such it should not be required to fast. Neither should parents compel their little children to fast. I have known children to cry for something to eat on fast day. In such cases, going without food will do them no good. Instead, they dread the day to come, and in place of hailing it, dislike it; . . . Better to teach them the principle, and let them observe it when they are old enough to choose intelligently, than to so compel them (*Gospel Doctrine*, pp. 243-244).

When training children to fast, the principle should first be explained to them. When abstinence is begun, missing one meal may be sufficient at first, then lengthening the degree of abstaining from food and water until the twenty-four hour period is attained.

Prayer should be a necessary part of the preparation we make before the fast starts when we meet with our family and discuss the meaning and purpose of the fast. Families should unite their faith in a common goal and should pray not only before, but during, and at the conclusion of that fast.

Prayers during the fast period should come from the heart, with a purpose, full of humility and thanks. It is a time to petition the Lord for our righteous desires, for the healing of the sick, for the solution to family problems, for help in our callings. Expressions of appreciation for our lives, our families, our leaders, the gospel, our country are most appropriate.

The spirit we have during the fast is of primary importance. Fast Day cannot be a mechanical monthly process to get it over with, associated with great discomfort. The spirit of the Lord will pour down upon us if we have faith, humble ourselves, admit our dependence on the Lord, pray and love our fellow men.

> . . . If, during a fast, one does nothing but abstain from eating and drinking, then the total result is that he becomes physically hungry. The negative aspect of abstinence is of little value without the accompaniment of the spiritual exercises of fasting.
>
> Fasting is not meant to weaken the body unnecessarily but to strengthen the will. Growth's greatest problem is loss of control. Fasting aims at self-control (Alan P. Johnson, *Fasting, the Second Step to Eternal Life*).

Abstinence from food and drink proves that we can be the master of our own body. We improve our self-control and open the way for the spirit to be with us. Some live the law of the fast except for the observance of the twenty-four hour time period. We want to live all of the law and gain all the blessings therefrom.

When we fast properly, we gain strength of character and learn to control our appetites, our passions, and our tempers. Concerning these controls, Alan P. Johnson, in his book, *Fasting, the Second Step to Eternal Life*, explains:

> Fasting represents an attitude of detachment from the things which gratify man temporarily, whether it be from

food, pleasure, marital cohabitation, or lawful ambition. It is a mental discipline which constructs a competent personality and character. . . . It applies to everything which a man may desire. Fasting is really putting God first when one acts. It is wanting God more than wanting food or sleep; more than wanting fellowship with others; and more than wanting to attend to business.

When properly observed, fasting is a time to develop our spiritual powers. It is a time when we can draw nearer to our Heavenly Father. When we fast wisely and prayer-fully, we develop our faith, and with that increased faith, we can have greater spiritual power.

The leading principle object of the institution of the fast among the Latter-day Saints was that the poor might be provided with food and other necessities. It is, there-fore, incumbent upon every Latter-day Saint to give to his bishop, on fast day, the food that he or his family would consume for the day, that it may be given to the poor for their benefit and blessing; or, in lieu of the food, that it's equivalent amount, or, . . . a liberal donation, in money, be so reserved and dedicated to the poor. . . .

None are exempt from this; it is required of the Saints, old and young, in every part of the Church (Joseph F. Smith, *Gospel Doctrine*, pp. 243-244).

President Spencer W. Kimball has said:

Fast offerings have long constituted the means from which the needs of the Lord's poor have been provided. It has been, and now is, the desire and objective of the Church to obtain from fast offerings the necessary funds to meet the cash needs of the welfare program; and to obtain from welfare production projects the commodity needs. If we give a generous fast offering, we shall in-crease our own prosperity both spiritually and temporally (*Ensign*, Nov. 1977, p. 79).

President Kimball has also counseled the saints, saying: "I think we should . . . give, instead of the amount saved by our two meals of fasting, perhaps much, much more — ten times more when we are in a position to do it" (*Conference Report*, Oct. 1974, p. 184).

The law of the fast is a principle with a promise, when lived by the proper spirit. It blesses both giver and receiver. Upon practicing the law of the fast, one finds strength to overcome self-indulgence and selfishness.

* * *

Fast offerings are just one way to be of service to others in the welfare services program of the Church. Welfare services include the spiritual, physical and emotional well-being of each child of God.

"Latter-day Saints . . . should take care of their own material needs and then contribute to the welfare of those who cannot provide the necessities of life. If a member is unable to sustain himself, then he is to call upon his own family, and then upon the Church, in that order." (Boyd K. Packer, "Self-Reliance," *Ensign*, Aug. 1975, p. 85).

We must be willing to serve our fellowmen, no matter what our income, age, condition of health, or social position. Through our service to others, we increase our ability to love, and we become less selfish.

The Savior provided the perfect example of service. He explained that he didn't come to earth to be served but to serve and to give his life for us (see Matthew 20:28). The Savior's life on earth reflected his pure love for mankind. Charity is that pure love of Christ in our lives when we, from the heart, show genuine concern and compassion for all our brothers and sisters (see John 3:16-24).

In the *Book of Mormon*, the prophet Moroni tells us: "Wherefore cleave unto charity, which is the greatest of all, for all things must fail — but charity is the pure love of Christ, and it endureth forever. . . .

"Pray unto the father with all the energy of heart, that ye may be filled with this love (charity), which he hath bestowed upon all who are true followers of his Son, Jesus Christ" (Moroni 7:46-48).

We can give money, food, or other articles to those who need them. We can be a friend to a newcomer. We can plant a garden or clean a yard of an elderly person or care for someone who is sick or comfort someone who grieves. President Spencer W. Kimball has explained: "God does notice us, and he watches over us. But it is usually through another person that he meets our needs" (*Ensign*, Dec. 1974, p. 5).

God blesses us with talents and abilities to help improve the lives of others. The services we select to do for others should be performed in a quiet, unheralded way, without seeking acclaim and without thought for reward or reciprocation. Albert Pipe once said: "What we have done for ourselves alone dies with us. What we have done for others and the world remains and is immortal."

If we turn our back upon those who are destitute and sick, or need help in any way, it is just as if the Savior had come asking for those things and we had turned him away. The Lord said: "Inasmuch as ye have done it unto the least of these my brethren, ye have done it unto me" (Matthew 25:34-40).

As King Benjamin said in the *Book of Mormon* concerning service we render in behalf of the welfare of others: "When ye are in the service of your fellow beings ye are only in the service of your God" (Mosiah 2:17).

Home Production & Storage   **11**

☐   *Store a year's supply of food and non-food essentials; plant a garden; become self-sustaining.*

"Let every head of household see to it that he has on hand enough food and clothing, and where possible, fuel also, for at least a year ahead" (J. Reuben Clark, Jr., *Conference Report*, Apr. 1937, p. 26).

The Church of Jesus Christ teaches independence, industry, thrift and self-reliance. The Apostle Paul wrote in the New Testament: "But if any provide not for his own and specially for those of his own house, he hath denied the faith . . ." (I Tim. 5:8).

Home production and storage is but one of the six elements of personal and family preparedness emphasized by the Church so that Latter-day Saints may be better prepared to meet the ordinary day-to-day requirements of successful living.

The meaning of family preparedness was explained by H. Burke Peterson, then of the Presiding Bishopric: "When we speak of family preparedness, we should speak of forseen, anticipated, almost expected needs which can be met through wise preparation. Even true emergencies can be modified by good planning" ("The Family in Welfare Serve," Welfare Services meeting, April 1975, p. 4).

A home production and storage program should be undertaken according to the needs of the individual or family. Each person or family should produce as much as possible through gardening, sewing, and making household items, and by learning techniques of home canning, freezing and drying foods, and where legally permitted, store and save a one-year supply of food, clothing, and if possible, fuel.

Although the application may vary in different locations and circumstances, the responsibility for preparedness remains. President Spencer W. Kimball has outlined the basic responsibilities of preparedness:

> Recognizing that the family is the basic unit of both the Church and society generally; we call upon Latter-day Saints everywhere to strengthen . . . with renewed effort in these specific areas: *food production, preservation, storage; the production and storage of non-food items*. . .
>
> We encourage you to grow all the food that you feasibly can on your own property. Berry bushes, grapevines, fruit trees — plant them if your climate is right for their growth. Grow vegetables and eat them from your own yard. Even those residing in apartments or condominiums can generally grow a little food in pots and planters. Study the best methods of providing your own foods. Make your garden . . . neat and attractive as well as productive. If there are children in your home, involve them in the process with assigned responsibilities. . . .
>
> Wherever possible, produce your nonfood necessities of life. Improve your sewing skills; sew and mend clothing for your family . . . Develop handicraft skills . . . , and make or build needed items ("Family Preparedness," *Ensign*, May 1976, pp. 124-125).

A well managed garden and preservation system is one of the best guarantees against economic hardship that a family could have. Where there is a will, there is a way in having a garden, no matter how small a space there is available. If the principle is lived, the Lord will bless the harvest and the soul.

Our church leaders have counseled us for many years in producing our own food as reviewed in the following statements:

> We have asked everyone wherever possible to assist with a home garden for the production of food so you may enjoy the efforts of your labors and help provide for your needs. We urge parents not only to engage in this activity, but to let their boys and girls share in helping with the garden. They will not only learn the value and joy of work, but it will help them develop a sense of responsibility as they participate in such family projects (Spencer W. Kimball, "Hold Fast to the Iron Rod". *Ensign,* Nov. 1978, p. 4).
>
> . . . Grow all the food you possibly can. Also remember to buy a year's supply of garden seeds so that, in case of shortage, you will have them for the following spring (Vaughn J. Featherstone, *Ensign,* May 1976, pp. 116).
>
> . . . We will see the day when we will live on what we produce (Marion G. Romney, *Conference Report,* April 1975, p. 165).

Food preservation and storage is one of the most important aspects of home production. The best method to use in preserving any fresh food for storage is determined by such factors as the nature of the food itself, space and equipment available, climate, other storage conditions, and cost.

There are several methods of food preservation such as:

1. Drying
2. Smoking and curing
3. Salting
4. Sugar preserving
5. Canning or bottling
6. Bin Storage

7. Cold storage and   8. Fermenting and pickling
   freezing

The production of non-food items is just as important in the total production program. In order to become independent and to stimulate industry and thrift, individuals and families should develop skills in making and producing nonfood essentials. Home production of nonfood items might include: *quilt-making, clothing production, soap-making, fuel production, and furniture-making.*

Planned storage in the home can help us as individuals and families to be self-sustaining in whatever situation we meet. Accident, illness, unemployment, or commodity shortage may affect any family at any time. Wars, depressions, famines, earthquakes, floods, and tornadoes are also possibilities to consider in planning for the care and protection of the family.

In *April 1937*, President J. Reuben Clark, Jr. counseled that the saints should save in times of plenty for emergencies in the lean years. Now many years later, the prophets still are counseling the saints to do the same: "We encourage families to have on hand this year's supply; *and we say it over and over and over and repeat over and over the scripture of the Lord where He says, 'Why call ye me, Lord, Lord, and do not the things which I say?'* How empty it is as they put their spirituality, so called, into action and call him by his important names, but fail to do the things which he says" (Spencer W. Kimball, "Family Preparedness," *Ensign,* May 1976, p. 125).

Elder Harold B. Lee, in a welfare agricultural meeting on October 1, 1966, said:

> We have never laid down an exact formula for what anybody should store. . . . Perhaps if we think not in terms of a year's supply of what we ordinarily would use, and think more in terms of what it would take to

keep us alive in case we didn't have anything else to eat, that last would be very easy to put in storage for a year. . . . If you think in terms of that kind of annual storage rather than a whole year's supply of everything that you are accustomed to eat, which, in most cases, is utterly impossible for the average family, I think we will come nearer to what President Clark advised us way back in 1937 ("Storage Problems," p. 76).

As to the foodstuffs which should be stored, the Church has left that decision primarily to us as individuals ourselves. There are three categories of home storage: 1) *Basic storage;* 2) *Emergency storage;* and 3) *Expanded storage.* Basic storage will be the only program treated here.

Basic storage includes life-sustaining foods and nonfood items that will store reasonably well for long periods. A one-year supply should include:

Basic Four Food Essentials —

1. *Wheat* (300 lbs./person) and other cereal grains.
2. *Non-fat powdered milk* (75 lbs./person)
3. *Sugar or Honey* (60 lbs./person)
4. *Salt* (5 lbs./person)

Other Essentials —

1. *Water* (minimum two-weeks supply-14 gallons/person)
2. *Garden Seeds*
3. *Basic emergency items* (rope, flashlights, matches, candles, etc.)
4. *Medical supplies* (basic first aid and cleaning items stored in water-tight containers)
5. *Clothing and bedding.*
6. *Fuel for cooking and warmth* (coal, wood, etc.)

Food storage can be stored in a number of unique places if there is limited space available, for example:

closets, attics, space under beds, or putting table cloths over boxes of food storage to make end tables and other furniture.

Storage should be acquired according to an orderly and systematic plan consistent with the family's needs. Borrowing money to acquire food is discouraged. Food costs can be minimized by budgeting properly and shopping wisely. Store foods that the family is willing to eat. In times of stress, it may be difficult to eat unfamiliar or disliked foods.

Stored foods should be used and replaced on a regular basis to maintain quality and minimize waste. Maintain a food inventory control sheet and replace items as they are used.

Security through home production and storage can be strengthened if members of the Church live righteously, avoid debt, practice thrift, and are willing to work. A family committed to these steps may be able to eat home-grown fresh product during the summer, *and* the winter; eat their bottled fruit and vegetables harvested and preserved; buy good quality clothing, fabric, and shoes at store sales, flea markets and garage sales; and be blessed by repairing, improving, altering and building useful items within the home to save costs and learn the value of self-sufficiency and work.

The Lord has said, "All things unto me are spiritual, and not at any time have I given unto you a law which was temporal" (D&C 29:24).

President Spencer W. Kimball has reminded us, saying:

> Some have become casual about keeping up their year's supply of commodities. . . . Should evil times come, many might wish they had filled all their fruit bottles and cultivated a garden in their backyards and planted a few fruit trees and berry bushes and provided for their own commodity needs.

The Lord planned that we would be independent of every creature . . . (*Ensign,* Nov. 1974, pp. 6-7).

President Kimball has further stated:

Let's do these things because they are right, because they are satisfying, and because we are obedient to the counsels of the Lord. In this spirit we will be prepared for most eventualities, and the Lord will prosper and comfort us. It is true that difficult times will come — for the Lord has foretold them — and, yes, stakes of Zion are "for a defense, and for a refuge from the storm." (D&C 115:6.) But if we live wisely and providently, we will be as safe as in the palm of His hand (Conference address, *Ensign,* Nov. 1977, p. 78).

(Note: An inexpensive resource guide published by the Church, *Essentials in Home Production and Storage,* No. PGWE1125) is available from Church Distribution. This basic reference workbook not only provides excellent information on the subject of storage, but it can also be used as an inventory control checklist for commodities stored.)

Tithes and Offerings/ Financial Management 12

☐ *Establish financial goals; pay honest tithes and offerings; avoid debt; save regularly and wisely use economic resources.*

> *"We must first seek the kingdom (of God), work and plan and spend wisely, plan for the future, and use what wealth we are blessed with to help build up the kingdom."* — President N. Eldon Tanner ("Constancy Amid Change", *Ensign*, Nov. 1979, p. 81).

Prosperity is our divine heritage as a child of God. It is our right to be prosperous. God has promised us in I Cor. 3:21 that, "all things are yours" but we should be mindful to ask Him for divine guidance about all our affairs, including our financial ones.

Wealth means "abundant living" which is our spiritual right that we all should be working towards. In Deuteronomy 8:18 the Lord instructed Moses to remind the children of Israel, "But thou shalt remember the Lord thy God: for it is he that giveth thee power to get wealth".

We have oft heard the quote, "Ye cannot serve God and Mammon" (Matt. 6:24). People serve mammon who leave God out of their financial affairs and try to go it alone. In the *Book of Mormon*, the prophet Jacob gives us important counsel on this matter:

"But *before* ye seek for riches, seek ye first the kingdom of God.

"And after ye have obtained a hope in Christ ye shall obtain riches, *if ye seek them;* and ye will seek them for the intent to do good — to clothe the naked, and to feed the hungry, and to liberate the captive, and to administer relief to the sick and the afflicted" (Jacob 2:18-19; italics added).

The leaders of the Church have outlined goals in the financial and resource management area of the Personal and Family Preparedness program for the saints as follows:

1. Pay a full and honest tithe and offerings.
2. Properly budget your money.
3. Live within your income.
4. Plan major purchases, avoiding credit purchases.
5. Work toward home ownership.
6. Get out of debt.
7. Provide financial security for times of disability and advanced age.
8. Have a savings plan.
9. Take better care of your possessions.
10. Complete a will and initiate estate planning.

The first principle of the gospel is faith in God. The real test of that recognition is giving. We consecrate our lives in this Church to the advancement of the cause of God. There is no higher evidence of that consecreation than this giving which has been commanded us by the Lord.

The law of tithing is a law of sacrifice, a celestial law calculated to test the strength of individual commitment. It is genuine worship and true recognition of the sovereignty of God.

The Lord said: "And this shall be the beginning of the tithing of my people. And after that those who have thus been tithed shall pay one-tenth of all their interest annually, and this shall be a standing law unto them forever" (D&C 119:4).

Paying our tithes does not represent giving gifts to the Lord and the Church. Paying tithing is discharging a *debt* to the Lord. The Lord is the source of all our temporal and spiritual blessings, including life itself. If we keep this commandment, the Lord promises we will "prosper in the land." Not only of material goods, but good health and vigor of mind, family unity and spiritual power. We cannot affort NOT to pay our tithes and offerings!

In Leviticus 27:32 we read: "The tenth shall be holy unto the Lord." The word "tithe" denotes a tenth part of our increase annually to the service of God. Those who do not contribute a full and honest tithe are literally robbing God and their own salvation, for the Lord said:

> *"Will a man rob God? Yet ye have robbed me. But ye say, wherein have we robbed thee? In tithes and offerings.*
> *"Bring ye all the tithes into the storehouse, that there may be meat in mine house, and prove me now herewith, saith the Lord of hosts, if I will not open you the windows of heaven, and pour you out a blessing, that there shall not be room enough to receive it"* (Malachi 3:8, 10).

As long as one is honest with the Lord, the amount of tithing paid is not material. Be absolutely honest with the Lord. President Heber J. Grant once said, "I believe that when a man is in financial difficulty the best way to get out of that difficulty is to be absolutely honest with the Lord and never allow a dollar to come into our hands without the Lord receiving ten percent of it."

"Every man who pays his tithing should enjoy paying it. The gospel of Christ is a gospel of enjoyment. 'Men are that they might have joy' as quoted in 2 Nephi 2:25. When one pays his tithing without enjoyment, he is robbed of a part of the blessing. He must learn to give cheerfully, willingly, and joyfully, and his gift will be blessed." (Stephen L. Richards, *The Law of Tithing*, pamphlet, p. 5.)

The Apostle Paul taught: "Let him give; not grudgingly, or of necessity: for God loveth a cheerful giver" (2 Cor. 9:6-7).

There is an important distinction between tithes and offerings. Even though tithing observance must be willing and voluntary, tithe-paying is nevertheless required, demanded in fact, by the Lord of his covenant people. Fast offerings are funds used to provide shelter, clothing, food and medical care to those who are in need, and relief to disaster-stricken members as well as others who cannot help themselves. Tithing funds help pay for the physical facility needs, such as heating and lighting for chapels; also supplies, activities, etc. for local church needs; new chapels, stake centers and temples, and welfare farm operations.

Funds from tithes are also directed to the operating of Church schools, seminaries, and institutions; the printing and distribution of church manuals and supplies, etc.; and genealogy research programs world-wide.

Other offerings may be given to the General Missionary Fund and the Family-to-Family Book of Mormon program to assist the ever-increasing growth of the Church.

Budgeting our money is an art. It isn't the earning of money that is hard to do, it's the management of that money.

President N. Eldon Tanner has said: "I have discovered that there is no way that you can ever earn more than you can spend. I am convinced that it is not the amount of money an individual earns that brings peace of mind as much as it is having *control* of his money. Money can be an obedient servant but a harsh taskmaster" (*Constancy Amid Change*, pamphlet, pp. 5-6).

We are counseled to budget our income and outgo and do not live beyond our means. It is difficult to control our "wants" if we consistently spend more than we earn. "One sure way to make life miserable is to live in a manner that you can't afford". (Richard L. Evans, *Quote Book*, p. 228.)

President Heber J. Grant once remarked: "If there is any one thing that will bring peace and contentment into the human heart, and into the family, it is to live within our means. And if there is any one thing that is grinding and discouraging and disheartening, it is to have debts and obligations that one cannot meet" (*Gospel Standards*, comp. G. Homer Durham, p. 111).

Family budgeting is essentially a matter of planning, not bookkeeping. It should be a guide to spending and in setting priorities in which will-power and discipline is applied. A sound budget plan is designed to keep one out of financial trouble, using the principle of thrift and careful planning. Using a simple income and expense ledger is very helpful. (Note: these ledgers are available at most drug and office supply stores).

It is all too easy to obtain instant credit nowadays. Elder O. Leslie Stone has said: "We are all being urged to 'buy now and pay later.' This makes it sound easy and even glamorous to surround ourselves with luxuries before they are earned. My advice to all is to *save now and buy later.* This will not only save a high interest charge, but it will also keep couples out of financial bondage" (*Ensign*, May 1978, p. 57).

The key to living within our means is discipline. Learning to distinguish between needs and desires is very important. Sacrifice is necessary sometimes in order to keep from spending more than is earned. Pres. J. Reuben Clark once said: "Let us avoid debt as we would avoid a plague; where we are now in debt let us get out of debt; if not today, then tomorrow. Let us straitly live within our incomes, and save a little" (*Conference Report*, Apr. 1937, p. 26.)

The Lord said: "Verily I say unto you, concerning your debts — behold it is my will that you shall pay all your debts" (D&C 104:78). And again: "Pay the debt thou hast contracted. . . . Release thyself from bondage" (D&C 19:35).

We cannot allow ourselves to dwell on things that we don't have money for. Instead of buying on credit, make major purchases with cash and enjoy it knowing it's paid for while saving for the next purchase. This is the key to freedom from debt. It can become a way of life that can bring quite a bit of peace into a home.

After paying the Lord His share, we should pay ourselves no less than ten percent of our income for the purpose of savings. Brigham Young counseled: "If you wish to get rich, save what you get. A fool can earn money; but it takes a wise man to save and dispose of it to his own advantage" (*Discourses of Brigham Young*, sel. John A. Widtsoe, Deseret Book Co., 1941, p. 292).

"Victor Hugo said: 'Above all, teach the children to save. Economy is the sure foundation for all virtues' . . . I feel sure that he who pays his tithes not only has a better conception of economy, but he is indulging in a practice that will bring him into better thrift habits and enable him to go forward toward financial prosperity." (Stephen L. Richards, *The Law of Tithing* pamphlet, p. 4).

Each child in the family should have a savings bank or savings account. This type of training can be a great motivation to save and to spend wisely. Short and long-range savings plans for missions, college programs, and marriage can be started early in life which can become a well-deserving financial habit.

There are many worthwhile ways to saving money in order to live within our means in these inflationary times. Some examples are: planting garden plots for food, sewing and mending clothing to make them last longer, limiting instead of purchasing a huge wardrobe, shopping with coupons, taking advantage of store sales, installing energy-saving insulation, lowering thermostats, and using common sense before running to the doctor for every little ailment, etc. Other ideas can be brought up in a family council meeting so that all can participate in saving money.

It is wise to have at least three months salary in savings at all times for an emergency or "rainy day" fund. Nothing seems so certain as to the unexpected in our lives. This is a plus factor that would keep a family stable in times of need and free from bondage of debt.

After the before-mentioned basics of financial management are met, we should, by frugal management, regularly save to create funds for investment. President N. Eldon Tanner has advised: "Investment debt should be fully secured so as not to encumber a family's security. Do not invest in speculative ventures. The spirit of speculation can become intoxicating. Many fortunes have been wiped out by the uncontrolled appetite to accumulate more and more" (*Ensign,* Nov. 1979, p. 82).

President Spencer W. Kimball has given this thought-provoking counsel:

> The Lord has blessed us as a people with a prosperity unequaled in times past. The resources that have been placed in our power are good, and necessary to our work here on the earth. But I am afraid that many of us have been surfeited with flocks and herds and acres and barns and wealth and have begun to worship them as false gods, and they have power over us. . . . Many people spend most of their time working in the service of a self-

image that includes sufficient money, stocks, bonds, investment portfolios, property, credit cards, furnishings, automobiles, and the like to *guarantee* carnal security throughout, it is hoped, a long and happy life. Forgotten is the fact that our assignment is to use these many resources in our families and quorums to build up the kingdom of God (*Ensign*, June 1976, p. 4).

Happiness and peace of mind have never increased with the amassing of property beyond the reasonable wants and needs of the family.

(Note: Two excellent sources for financial management and goal planning are: *Constancy Amid Change*, pamphlet, by N. Eldon Tanner, Church publication No. PBCT 1025; and *Latter Day Bondage, An LDS Guide to Personal Finance* by C. Douglas Beardall, LDS Book Publications).

Educational and Career Development   13

☐ *Take advantage of public educational and cultural opportunities; read good literature; develop and improve job skills.*

> *"Seek ye diligently and teach one another words of widsom; yea, seek ye out of the best books words of wisdom; seek learning, even by study and also by faith"* (D&C 88:118).

The Lord has revealed to us that we cannot be saved in ignorance. He has also told us that we *can* become perfect, even as our Father in Heaven is perfect (see Matt. 5:48).

Modern revelation has also inspired us that "the glory of God is intelligence, or, in other words, light and truth" (D&C 93:36). We gain light and truth in this life by seeking knowledge by prayer, study, and taking advantage of public and other educational and cultural opportunities.

In our family home evenings, we can develop specific short range goals to expand the mind for each member of the family, being consistent with each one's ability to learn something new. Examples might be from learning to tie a shoe for younger children to learning a scripture or song for the older children.

Other priorities for educational betterment might be:

1. Showing interest by helping children with their school work — checking their homework and providing additional research assistance such as using encyclopedias, etc. This encourages children to work hard and to succeed in doing a good job.

2. Latter-day Saint individuals and families should be aware of what is going on in the world. Parents should keep their eyes open for articles in the newspaper that would be of interest to their children, and perhaps discuss those issues of interest in conversation at the dinner table.

3. We speak of literacy and education in terms of being prepared for a better occupation, but we cannot underestimate the present pleasure of our reading in the scriptures, Church magazines, and good books of every kind. Plan and undertake a reading program of uplifting, outstanding literature. The selection of books may reflect a variety of interests or may emphasize one particular theme.

4. Visiting the local library regularly can be a tremendous asset to the family educationally. Reading good books regularly is inspiring and uplifting for the soul.

5. Field trips, special seminars, and courses provided by educational institutions and the community are helpful if taken full advantage of.

6. Obtaining a copy of the Standard Works of the Church for each member of the family wherein each may participate in regular family and personal scriptural study for spiritual development.

7. Development of a new interest in any creative field, such as: poetry, fiction writing, composition of music, art, dance, crafts, photography, drama, etc., or a hobby. Emphasis should be in an area that is new to our life.

8. Attendance at cultural events that will uplift and refine the mind, such as: musicals and dramatical plays, art shows, dance theatre, concerts, and visiting museums of various different artifacts, etc.

Concerning career development in our lives, "each head of household should select a suitable vocation or profession and pursue appropriate training" (*Personal and Family Preparedness*, pamphlet, Church Publication No. PGWE1191).

On-the-job training can be the best work development experience in life if taken advantage of with the right attitude and a willingness to learn. This type of career development is never-ending. Updated technology, new skills and methods are part of our changing and progressive world. As Latter-day Saints, we should not be satisfied with our present status, but should be striving to increase our technical capacity in our daily bread-winning labors.

To be successful in life spiritually, mentally, and temporally, it requires constant development of skills. Attendance at training programs and special seminars should be given every consideration when the opportunity is made available.·

Each child in a family should receive counsel to help him select a career that will satisfy family economic needs and provide personal satisfaction. The Scouting and Exploring programs of the Boy Scouts of America are excellent opportunities for young men to be exposed to numerous career interest areas. There are many opportunities for young girls at home to learn homemaking skills such as sewing, cooking or baking, and cleaning techniques. The girls should be given career educational opportunities also, just as the boys are given.

We should try not to prejudice children against certain jobs, classifying them as undesirable, but encourage them to find something that is useful and that they enjoy. Children should be taught that nothing comes without hard work, and that a job has to be done well — it's best to do more than is expected.

If we diligently try to improve ourselves in this life by

prayer, study, and works, the Lord promises us a blessing of great worth: "And all saints who remember to keep and do these sayings, walking in obedience to the commandments . . . shall find widsom and great treasures of knowledge, even hidden treasures" (D&C 89:18-19).

☐ *Observe the Word of Wisdom; maintain proper weight and a physical fitness program; practice preventive health care.*

"If we will clothe ourselves with bodies purified through observance of the Word of Wisdom, the destroying angels will pass us by, as they did the children of Israel." — President Marion G. Romney (*Ensign*, May 1979, p. 40).

We have come to this earth to gain a physical body in order that we may become like our Father in Heaven. Therefore, our body is a temple of God and should be taken care of properly.

From the beginning, the Lord has counseled man concerning good health and what he should or should not take into his body (see Genesis 1:29-30). In these latter days, the Lord revealed his law of health through the Prophet Joseph Smith. This revelation is the Word of Wisdom (see D&C 89). It is a valuable temporal law as well as a great spiritual law. President Stephen L. Richards offered this explanation concerning the spiritual impact of the Word of Wisdom:

Every commandment of God is spiritual in nature. . . . The Word of Wisdom is spiritual . . . the largest measure of good derived from its observance is in increased faith and the development of more spiritual power and wisdom. Likewise, the most regrettable and damaging effects of its infractions are spiritual, also. Injury to the body may be comparatively trivial to the damage to the soul in the destruction of faith and the retardation of spiritual growth. So I say, every commandment involves a spiritual growth (*Conference Report*, April 1949, p. 141).

Elder Theodore M. Burton has said:

I do know that God has counseled us not to use alcoholic beverages, tea, or coffee, and has told us not to use tobacco. How unwise it is to use any substance which is *habit forming* and harmful to the body. . . . I urge you, then to listen carefully to these words of warning, not only to avoid the use of those things which are harmful to your bodies, but also to use those foods recommended by the Lord with prudence and thanksgiving (*Ensign*, May 1976, p. 29).

The revelation of the Word of Wisdom specified certain substances that we should not take into our bodies. Are they the only ones we should not partake of? No. President Spencer W. Kimball has said, "We hope our people will eliminate from their lives all kinds of drugs so far as possible. Too many depend upon drugs as tranquilizers and sleep helps, which is not always necessary . . . we deplore such" (*Ensign*, Nov. 1974, p. 6).

We have been taught by the Lord that there are many good things for the body ordained for the constitution, nature, and use of man. The Lord has given us good herbs, fruits and grains. These are to be main foods of men and beasts. But we should not overlook the fact that they are to be used with "prudence and thanksgiving". In the 59th section of the *Doctrine and Covenants*, we are told that these things are not to be used "to excess, neither by extortion" (vs. 20). The difficulty with most of the human family, is eating too much and that is not good for the body functions. We should heed the counsel of the Lord and eat only wholesome foods and eat with prudence.

President Ezra Taft Benson has said: "We should use moderation in all good things. In general, the more food we eat in its natural state and the less it is refined without additives, the healthier it will be for us. Food can affect the mind, and deficiencies in certain elements in the body can promote mental depression" (*Ensign*, Nov. 1974, p. 66).

The Word of Wisdom encompassess more than taking in harmful substances into the body. *It is a complete law of health which includes the areas of work, cleanliness, proper rest and exercise.* The following are suggestions in maintaining good physical health:

1. *Maintain proper weight and endurance* through regular exercise, adequate rest, and balanced diet. ". . . cease to sleep longer than is needful; retire to thy bed early, that ye may not be weary; arise early, that your bodies and your minds may be invigorated" (D&C 88:124). Rest and physical exercise are essential to good health. A walk in the fresh air can refresh the spirit, and wholesome recreation can bring a change of pace in our lives. The recommended hours of sleep for adults is 7-8 hours and young children, 10-12 hours. To help reach a higher level of health, a physical fitness program should be established to fit the need.

2. *Practice sound principles in food selection and preparation.* It is recommended that families should eat three vegetables and two fruits daily for a balanced diet. Avoid "junk foods". Rely on fresh foods and whole grain cereals. Eat a good breakfast and start the day off with plenty of energy.

3. *Maintain personal and home cleanliness.*

4. *Practice sound principles of immunization and other preventive medical and dental care.* Accurate records should be kept.

5. *Acquire skills in first aid and home nursing.*

6. *Practice sound principles of sanitation and accident prevention.*

The Lord promises to bless us physically and spiritually if we keep his law of health and obey his other commandments:

> *And all saints who remember to keep and do these sayings, walking in obedience to the commandments, shall receive health in their navel and marrow to their bones;*
>
> *And shall find wisdom and great treasures of knowledge, even hidden treasures;*
>
> *And shall run and not be weary, and shall walk and not faint.*
>
> *And I, the Lord, give unto them a promise, that the destroying angel shall pass by them, as the children of Israel, and not slay them. (D&C 89:18-21).*

The promise of "hidden treasure" is a testimony of the divinity of the gospel of Jesus Christ, which comes as a result of obedience to the laws of God. We will be freed from the "destroying angel" of spiritual death, "For observing the Word of Wisdom the reward is life, not only prolonged mortal life but life eternal" (Spencer W. Kimball, *Miracle of Forgiveness*, p. 211).

☐ *Seek moral cleanliness in thought, word and action; maintain proper grooming standards; practice self-restraint; develop and maintain good manners.*

"Wherefore take unto you the whole armour of God, that ye may be able to withstand in the evil day, and having done all, to stand" (Ephesians 6:13).

Social-emotional and spiritual strength is one of the six areas in the Personal and Family Preparedness program of the welfare services of the Church. The goals in the program read:

Each person should build spiritual strength to meet life's challenges and stresses with confidence and stability by learning to love God and communicate with him in personal prayer, by learning to love and serve his neighbor, and by learning to love and respect himself through righteous living and self-mastery. Each family should understand that social-emotional and spiritual strength is a blessing that results from obedience to revealed princples of family living (*Personal and Family Preparedness Standards*, stock no. PGWE1191).

None of us have attained perfection or the zenith of spiritual growth that is possible in mortality. Every person can and must make spiritual progress in order to gain eternal life and exaltation. The gospel of Jesus Christ is the divine plan for that spiritual growth eternally.

Elder Howard W. Hunter has stated:

Developing spirituality and attuning ourselves to the highest influences of godliness is not an easy matter. It takes time and frequently involves a struggle. It will not happen by chance, but is accomplished only through deliberate effort and by calling upon God and keeping his commandments.

Part of our difficulty as we strive to acquire spirituality is the feeling that there is much to do and that we are falling far short. Perfection is something yet ahead for every one of us; but we can capitalize on our strengths, begin where we are, and seek after the happiness that can be found in pursuing the things of God. We should remember the Lord's counsel:

'Wherefore, be not weary in well-doing, for ye are laying the foundation of a great work. And out of small things proceedeth that which is great.

'Behold, the Lord requireth the heart and a willing mind; . . .' (D&C 64:33-34). ("Developing Spirituality", *Ensign*, May 1979, p. 25).

We are the sum of the thoughts we think; of the habits we have, of all we do and have done. We are the sum of all our actions and attitudes and utterances; of all things stored in mind and memory. The laws given by a loving Heavenly Father are always in force and always effective. His advice is worth taking, his commandments worth keeping.

President David O. McKay explained: "God gave man part of his divinity. He gave man the power of choice, and no other creature in the world has it. So he placed upon the individual the obligation of conducting himself as an eternal being. You cannot think of any greater gift that could come to a man or woman than the freedom of choice. You alone are responsible, and by wielding and exercising that freedom of choice, you grow in character, you grow in intelligence, you approach divinity, and eventually you may achieve that high exaltation" (*Conference Report*, Oct. 1969, pp. 6-7).

The Prophet Joseph Smith has given us an insight on the need to become spiritual and the time and patience which we must recognize are part of the process:

> We consider that God has created man with a mind capable of instruction, and a faculty which may be enlarged in proportion to the heed and diligence given to the light communicated from heaven to the intellect; and that the nearer man approaches perfection, the clearer are his views, and the greater his enjoyment, till he has overcome the evils of his life and lost every desire for sin; and like the ancients, arrives at the point of faith where he is wrapped in the power and glory of his Maker, and is caught up to dwell with Him. But we consider that this is a station to which no man ever arrived in a moment (*History of the Church*, 2:8.)

The fall of Adam brought each of us into a mortal condition in which we must struggle daily between inclinations toward good and inclinations toward evil. President David O. McKay has said, "the hardest battles of life are fought within the chambers of the soul" ("The Words of a Prophet", *Improvement Era*, Feb. 1970, p. 84).

The gospel teaches us that we in mortality are dual beings with both spiritual and fleshy inclinations and that we have the capacity for both righteousness and evil. The Savior hinted at the relationship of spirit and body and our tendencies when he said, "The spirit indeed is willing, but the flesh is weak" (Matthew 26:41).

President David O. McKay has said: "Man's earthly existence is but a test as to whether he will concentrate his efforts, his mind, his soul upon things which contribute to the comfort and gratification of his physical nature, or whether he will make as his life's purpose the acquisition of spiritual qualities" (*Improvement Era*, Dec. 1969, p. 31).

President McKay has given us an insight into the meaning of spirituality:

> Spirituality is the highest acquisition of the soul, "The divine in man — the supreme crowning gift that makes him king of all created things." It is the consciousness of victory over self, and of communion with the Infinite. To acquire more and more power, to feel one's faculties unfolding, and one's soul in harmony with God and with the Infinite — that is spirituality. It is that alone which really gives one the best in life (*True to the Faith*, pp. 245-45).

How do we develop and maintain spirituality of the quality that President David O. McKay has defined? We need to spend time reading the scriptures daily and reading only good uplifting literature; more meaningful communication with our Heavenly Father through daily personal and family prayers, morning and evening; repent of our wrongdoings; holding quality time for gospel discussion in our family home evening; attend Church meetings regularly and participate in Church activities; perform frequent acts of service to family members and others in need; double our performance in every calling in the Church; and being truly obedient to that which we have been asked to do.

To maintain the power of resistance from temptation, we need to not only apply these principles of the gospel in our lives, but put our trust in the Lord. A modern-day revelation makes this promise:

> Put your trust in that Spirit which leadeth to do good — yea, to do justly, to walk humbly, to judge righteously; and this is my Spirit.

> *Verily, verily, I say unto you, I will impart unto you my Spirit, which shall enlighten your mind, which shall fill your soul with joy;*
>
> *And then shall ye know, or by this shall you know, all things whatsoever you desire of me, which are pertaining unto things of righteousness, in faith believing in me that ye shall receive* (D&C 11:12-14).

Satan's plan is to deceive as many of us as he possibly can to prevent us from returning to live with our Heavenly Father. One of the most damaging things he can do is to entice us to break the law of chastity.

The law of chastity as the Lord has commanded his children to live by, is that *only* in marriage are we to have sexual relations with the one whom we are legally and lawfully wedded. We are to provide physical bodies for God's spirit children through sexual reproduction. This power of procreation is sacred to the Lord.

President Joseph F. Smith once stated: "The lawful association of the sexes is ordained of God, not only as the sole means of race perpetuation, but for the development of the higher faculties and nobler traits of human nature, which the love-inspired companionship of man and woman alone can insure" (*Improvement Era*, June 1917, p. 739).

Satan would like us to believe that it is no sin to break the law of chastity. He attacks our modesty, making us believe that because the body is beautiful, it should be seen and appreciated. He encouraged us to think immoral and improper thoughts, through pictures, movies, jokes, music and dance which suggest immoral acts.

The law of chastity requires that our thoughts as well as our actions be pure. Our minds become our greatest stewardship, since our thoughts control the physical body. Therefore being virtuous and chaste begins in the mind.

Elder Boyd K. Packer has stated:

Our thoughts are subject to influence from other sources — good and evil, both from without, from the physical and environmental world, and from sources within. . . .

Our thoughts are subject to spiritual influence. . . .

But, regardless of the influence, and regardless of the source, the most important consideration is that *we may choose*. We are free to choose ("Let Virtue Garnish Thy Thoughts," BYU *Speeches of the Year*, Sept. 26, 1967, p. 7).

President David O. McKay has said: "Man is endowed with appetites and passions for the preservation of his life and the perpetuation of his kind. These, when held under proper subjection, contribute to happiness and comfort, but when used for mere gratification, lead to misery and moral degradation" (*Treasures of Life*, p. 531).

From the beginning of the world, God has declared moral cleanliness to be one of the most important requirements for a happy life. Regarding the blessings of moral purity, the First Presidency has said: "How glorious is he who lives the chaste life. He walks unfearful in the full glare of the noonday sun, for he is without moral infirmity. . . . He is loved by the Lord, for he stands without blemish. The exhaltations of eternities await his coming" (Heber J. Grant, J. Reuben Clark, David O. McKay, *Improvement Era*, Nov. 1942, p. 759).

If children are to have wholesome attitudes and understanding about their own sexuality and the laws of virtue and chastity, they need to be properly educated by example and precept in the home. If we don't teach them, the world will!

As we teach chastity and virtue, our goals are to help our young people to first, understand the positive, lawful role of their physical desires and how to manage them and second, to *want* to be chaste and virtuous. Chastity is so important that President Spencer W. Kimball counseled young people to fight if necessary to protect it: "It is better to die in defending one's virtue than to live having lost it without a struggle" (*Miracle of Forgiveness*, p. 196).

President Kimball has also stated in a direct way the stand of the General Authorities of the Church against unchastity: "No indecent exposure of pornography or other aberrations to defile the mind and spirit. No fondling of bodies, one's own or that of others, and no sex between persons except in proper marriage relationships. . . . We affirm our strong, unalterable stand against unchastity in all its many manifestations" (*Ensign*, May 1974, pp. 7-8).

President David O. McKay summarized the gaining of spirituality in these words: "*Spirituality is best manifested in doing, not in dreaming.* 'Rapturous day dreams, flights of heavenly fancy, longings to see the invisible, are not so impressive as the plain doing of duty' " (*True to the Faith*, p. 245).

The following points are suggestions to assist individuals and families in keeping a chaste life and maintaining spirituality:

1. Keep literature in the home that is of the highest moral quality.
2. Do not allow off-color jokes or stories to be told in the home.
3. Control television viewing in the home so that questionable shows are avoided.
4. Teach good manners to each other by precept and example.
5. As parents, try to radiate wholesome attitudes toward lawful sexual behavior.
6. Do not support entertainment events of a questionable moral nature.

7. Discuss and exemplify appropriate behavior toward the opposite sex.

8. Teach the positive blessings of self-restraint; channel thoughts and the power of prayer and fasting in resisting temptation.

Magnify Callings/
Meeting Attendance   16

☐ *Attend all meetings regularly; magnify Church assignments.*

> *"Only the standard of excellence is the goal we should be attempting to achieve in the assignment we have been given in Church service . . . with diligence make every effort to achieve the highest level of performance"* — Elder L. Tom Perry (*Ensign*, May 1977, p. 61.)

Every individual member of the Church of Jesus Christ of Latter-day Saints has a special calling — being an active and exemplary representative of the Church, living the commandments of God, and assisting in the building of Zion in preparation for the Second Coming of the Savior.

God did not set up the Church for his own benefit, but for the benefit of his children. The Lord has provided his Church with the instructional means necessary to assist us as individual members and our family unit in the teaching, training, and edifying process for our perfection. This is accomplished through the established auxilliary programs and Priesthood quorums of the Church.

Meetings of the Primary organization for the children, Sunday School and Young Women's programs, Relief Society for the sister saints, as well as the Aaronic and Melchizedek Priesthood quorums for the worthy male membership over twelve years of age are held each week for the purpose of edifying all the members of the Church. Through regular attendance, we may learn more fully the ways of the Lord and what is expected of us.

Attendance at Sacrament meeting each Sabbath day is a commandment given to the Saints by the Lord (see D&C 59:9) wherein we renew our covenants with the Lord, whose name we have taken upon ourselves at the time of our baptism into the Church. By renewing covenants worthily each week with the Lord, he promises us the blessings of his Spirit to be with us.

As members we should also attend Stake and General Conferences of the Church where the word and counsel of the Lord is spoken by his servants, the General Authorities.

Many saints in the Church are called to leadership and teaching positions within the priesthood and auxilliary organizations to strengthen Zion. We are asked to continually magnify our callings. To magnify is to honor, to exalt and glorify; and "cause to be held in greater esteem or respect; to increase the importance of, to enlarge and make greater" (*Webster's Seventh Collegiate Dictionary*).

If we have special talents, we should use them to serve our fellowmen. God blesses us with talents and abilities to help improve the lives of others. We can accomplish this by doing missionary work, accepting assignments, visiting other church members, teaching classes and doing a variety of other church work. In the Church of Jesus Christ there is no professional clergy so we, as lay members, must carry on all of its activities.

Can members of the Church magnify their callings if they refuse to accept positions and responsibilities of trust when called upon to serve by those in authority, or refuse to sustain by faith, prayer and works those whom God has called and ordained to preside over them? Can a person magnify a calling who is not willing to sacrifice and consecrate all for the building of God's kingdom in righteousness, truth and power in the earth?

If a member finds himself failing to be amenable to the counsel and direction of righteous men who are properly called and approved by the Saints as authorized leaders, the reason is more than likely that he is not fully obedient to certain gospel standards and requirements and should re-evaluate his life and actions, for it is a sure step to the road of apostasy.

Our calling as a covenant people and as members of the Church of Jesus Christ of Latter-day Saints is a steward-ship. Stewardship is a sacred spiritual trust requiring accountability by the Lord. A faithful steward exercises righteous dominion and consecrates his time, talents and means to build the Lord's kingdom here on earth (see D&C 42:30; 104:11-18).

What blessings come when the priesthood is used properly? The Lord has promised great blessings to righteous priesthood holders who use the priesthood to bless others: "Then shall thy confidence wax strong in the presence of God; and the doctrine of the priesthood shall distil upon thy soul as the dews from heaven. The Holy Ghost shall be thy constant companion, and thy scepter an unchanging scepter of righteousness and truth; and thy dominion shall be an everlasting dominion, and without compulsory means it shall flow unto thee forever and ever" (D&C 121:45-46).

President David O. McKay made this promise to every man who faithfully used the priesthood in righteousness: "He will find his life sweetened, his discernment sharpened to decide quickly between right and wrong, his feelings tender and compassionate, yet his spirit strong and valiant in defense of right; he will find the priesthood a never-failing source of happiness — a well of living water springing up unto eternal life" (*Instructor*, Oct. 1968, p. 378).

There has never been a person who did not feel good inside for going the extra mile in helping another fellow human being in need. That is the essence of the home teaching and visiting teaching program of the Church. Elder L. Tom Perry has explained the sacredness of the calling and obligation in these programs:

> Beginning with father Adam down to the present when the Lord's church has been organized on the earth, there has been a system, a program to have brotherly and sisterly concern for one another. The history of these general conferences is filled with discourses from the Brethren reminding us of this sacred obligation. I have been impressed to add my voice to that record today with the hope that we can be motivated to place the calling of home teachers in its proper priority in our lives.
> . . . The family is the basic unit in the Church organization. The home teacher is the first line of defense to watch over and strengthen that basic unit. In our priority of time commitments we ought to first watch over and strengthen our own families, and then be good, consistent, conscientious home teachers.
> . . . If our home teaching assignments are to be given their proper priority, then our preparation for those visits must be careful and complete, tailored to the individual needs of fathers and mothers and their families. As home teachers, should not this basic program receive our earnest effort to seek inspiration and guidance of the Lord in this most sacred obligation? ("Home Teaching, A Sacred Calling," *Ensign,* Nov. 1978, p. 70-71).

Each member of the Church is a link to the success in building up the kingdom of God. Husbands and wives and families should support and encourage each other to help make church callings easier to bare. Magnifying one's calling will bring the blessings of a kind and loving Father in Heaven and will bring joy and happiness in this life and the life to come.

Work, Honesty and Integrity 17

☐ *Avoid idleness; give honest labor; practice the princi-ples of honesty and integrity in all aspects of life.*

"Work is to be re-enthroned as the ruling principle of the lives of our Church membership" — Heber J. Grant (*Conference Report*, Oct. 1936, p. 3).

Zion is built on the principle of love of God and fellow-man, work, and earnest labor, as God has directed. After the fall, God gave Adam his law of labor: ". . . in the sweat of thy face shalt thou eat bread" (see Genesis 3:19).

"Labor is the manufacturer of wealth. It is ordained of God, as the medium to be used by man to obtain his living: hence it is the universal condition of this great bond to live. . . ." (John Taylor, *Times and Seasons* 5:679, Oct. 15, 1844).

The Lord has said:

Behold, I say unto you that it is my will that you should go forth and not tarry, neither be idle but labor with your might. . . .

And again, verily I say unto you, that every man who is obliged to provide for his own family, let him provide, and he shall in nowise lose his crown; and let him labor. . . .

Let every man be diligent in all things. And the idler shall not have place in the church, except he repent and mend his ways. (D&C 75:3, 28-29).

In setting up the welfare program of the Church, the First Presidency said: "Our primary purpose was to set up, in so far as it might be possible, a system under which the curse of idleness would be done away with, the evils of a dole, abolished, and independence, industry, thrift, and self respect be once more established amongst our people. The aim of the Church is to help the people to help themselves" (*Conference Report*, Oct. 1936, p. 3).

Husbands who are physically able should provide food and shelter and other necessities for their wives and children. The Apostle Paul wrote: "If any provide not for his own, and specially for those of his own house, he hath denied the faith" (I Timothy 5:8).

Parents should start early in the lives of their children to teach them good working attitudes, habits and skills and to share work responsibilities in and around the home that fit their abilities.

Attitudes toward work is of most importance. President David O. McKay once said: "Let us realize that the *privilege to work* is a gift; that the *power to work* is a blessing; that the *love of work* is success" (quoted by Franklin D. Richards, "The Gospel of Work", *Improvement Era*, Dec. 1969, p. 103).

Work is the key to full joy in the plan of God, for "men are that they might have joy" (2 Nephi 2:25). There is no real division between spiritual, mental and physical work. Work is essential to each of us for growth in character, in development, and in a hundred satisfactions which the idle never know.

President Theodore Roosevelt said: "The happiest man is he who has toiled hard and successfully in his life work. The work may be done in a thousand different ways; with the brain or the hands, in the study, the field, or the work-shop; if it is honest work, honestly done and well worth doing, that is all we have a right to ask" (*A Nation of Pioneers*, quoted by Richard L. Evans, *Improvement Era*, Nov. 1963, p. 984).

Latter-day Saints are an industrious, self-sustaining people. Pride in work and giving honest labor are qualities that bring success and happiness.

President Heber J. Grant declared:

> I am a firm believer that work does not kill anyone. . . . Men should have a pride in doing their full share and never want to be paid for that which they have not earned. . . . I assert with confidence that the law of success, here and hereafter, is to have a humble and a prayerful heart, and to work, work, work. . . .
>
> I have been impressed with the fact that there is a spirit growing in the world today to avoid giving service, an unwillingness to give value received, to try to see how little we can do and how much we can get for doing it. This is all wrong. Our spirit and aim should be to do all we possibly can, in a given length of time, for the benefit of those who employ us and for the benefit of those with whom we are associated (*Gospel Standards, Improvement Era* Pub., 1941, pp. 108-109).

Concerning honesty in business, Elder L. Tom Perry said to fathers: ". . . be honest in your business dealings. Be loyal to your employers. Determine to be the best in your chosen field of endeavor. Each day make a full effort to be more productive than you were the day before. I challenge you to be leaders in your chosen professions and occupations" ("But Be Ye Doers of the Word", *Ensign*, May 1977, p. 61).

God condemns idleness and gain from evil and idle pursuits. President Spencer W. Kimball has stated: "I feel strongly that men who accept wages or salary and do not give . . . (fair) time, energy, devotion, and service are receiving money that is not clean. . . . Clean money is that . . . (pay) received for a full day's honest work." (*Conference Report*, Oct. 1953, p. 52.) We should not let the "something for nothing" idea to creep into our lives or the lives of our children. Nothing of value comes to us in this life without being earned properly.

The development of a high and noble character should be foremost in the pursuit of eternal excellence. It is earned by our honesty and integrity. Integrity, or the lack of it, touches almost every facet of our lives — everything we say, every thought and desire.

In the *Thirteenth Article of Faith* it reads: "We believe in being honest, true, chaste, benevolent, virtuous, and in doing good to all men; indeed, we may say that we follow the admonition of Paul — We believe all things, we hope all things, we have endured many things, and hope to be able to endure all things. If there is anything virtuous, lovely, or of good report or praiseworthy, we seek after these things."

Dishonesty threatens our personal integrity. It chokes our conscience, our character withers, our self-respect vanishes, our integrity dies. Dishonesty cheats one's soul. President Gordon B. Hinckley has said of cheating:

> . . . it robs virtue, it robs loyalty, it robs sacred promises, it robs self-respect, it robs truth. It involves deception. It is personal dishonesty of the worst kind, for it becomes a betrayal of the most sacred of human relationships. . . .
>
> We cannot be less than honest, we cannot be less than true, we cannot be less than virtuous if we are to keep sacred the trust given us. Once it was said among our people that a man's word was as good as his bond. Shall

any of us be less reliable, less honest that our forebearers? (*Ensign,* May 1976, pp. 61-62).

President N. Eldon Tanner gave this wise counsel concerning integrity:

Our children should value honesty and integrity. They should know and understand that they are children of God, and that their eternal destiny is to so live that they will be worthy to return to his presence when they have completed their life's mission. Adults should not hinder their progress, but help them always to be true to their ideals and principles. . . .

The integrity of which we speak is not impossible to attain. In fact, we should all be convinced that it is far easier to emulate the example of our Savior than it is to follow Satan, whose path leads us away from integrity and into darkness and misery. (*Ensign,* May 1977, pp. 16-17).

If there are ways in which we are being even the least bit dishonest, we should begin at once to repent of them. When we are completely honest, we cannot be corrupted. We are true to every trust, duty, agreement, or covenant even if it costs us money, friends, or our lives. Then we can face the Lord, ourselves, and others without shame.

President Joseph F. Smith counseled us: "Let every man's life be so that his character will bear the closest inspection, and that it may be seen as an open book, so that we will have nothing to shrink from or be ashamed of" (*Gospel Doctrine,* p. 252).

To maintain honesty and integrity the following suggestions can be incorporated into one's character for a lifetime:

1. Strive to apply the principle of the "second mile" in all dealings with mankind by doing more than is expected.

2. Live the Master's Golden Rule: "Do unto others as you would have others do unto you."

3. Make promises and commitments carefully. When they are made, count it as sacred words of honor, and act accordingly.

4. Seek to eliminate false pride.

5. Seek to be truthful in all that is said. Avoid gossip, no matter how small. Carefully consider speech to avoid hurting or offending others.

6. Be honest in all dealings and relationships, whether in business, Church, or at home. Take nothing that belongs to anyone else, no matter how small, without permission from the owner.

7. Do not envy others or seek by improper means to acquire that which belongs to others.

8. Keep sacred any confidences entrusted.

9. Develop a love for and dedication to honorable, hard work.

10. Be courageous enough to acknowledge mistakes, to apologize when appropriate, to make things right if given offense.

11. Cultivate friends and companions who are earnestly seeking to maintain high ideals.

Development of Natural Talents 18

☐ *Develop naturally-given talents; acquire greater pro-ficiency of a developed talent; use talents for the good of others.*

"That which we persist in doing becomes easier for us to do; not that the nature of the thing is changed, but that the power to do has increased". — Heber J. Grant (*Gospel Standards*, p. 335).

Each one of us has been blessed with a special talent in life. Sometimes we may think that we are not blessed with a talent and that others have been blessed with several abilities. That is not true. Our Heavenly Father blessed each one of us with certain abilities in the pre-existence and we brought them with us. These talents or abilities just need to be developed and should not be kept hidden away.

Having a special talent does not necessarily have to include being a great singer or having great sports abilities. We might be blessed with the ability to teach others, or have the quality of patience and the understanding of others.

Some people may have several noticable talents, but they were not given to them "on a silver platter" in one day. Those talents and abilities were developed with much determination, sacrifice and plain hard practice.

Sometimes the Lord gives us weakness so that we will overcome them. They will become our strengths, for the Lord said: "I give unto men weakness that they may be humble; and my grace is sufficient for all men that humble themselves before me; for if they humble themselves before me, and have faith in me, then will I make weak things become strong unto them" (Ether 12:27).

The Lord gave each one of us talents that could be put to use in building up his kingdom on earth. A talent is a stewardship in the kingdom that should be developed and made perfect to be used for the benefit of others. If our works are good, the Lord will bless us with other talents and responsibilities in the kingdom, and our reward will be increased. The Lord said: "Let your light so shine before men, that they may see your good works, and glorify your Father which is in heaven" (Matthew 5:16).

Concerning the use of talents, President Joseph F. Smith said: "Every son and daughter of God has received some talent, and each will be held to strict account for the use or misuse to which it is put" (*Juvenile Instructor*, Nov. 1903, p. 689).

Elder Robert E. Wells has given this insight to magnifying talents:

> The capacity the Lord looks for in us is that ability to perform to the degree that we become profitable servants unto him. The Lord has given us talents, gifts, and blessings. He expects us to magnify them and to use them in the service of others if he is to trust us.
>
> The servant who received five talents returned ten and received the praise 'Well done, thou good and faithful servant: thou hast been faithful over a few things, I will make thee ruler over many things' (Matthew 25:21). The servant who had received two talents returned four talents, and he received equal praise with the first. How-

ever, the Lord chastised the slothful servant that received one talent for not multiplying that which had been given to him. The principle is clear: The Lord likes to see capacity double; he likes to see his servants double that which has been given to them — in talents or in responsibilities. (*Ensign,* Nov. 1978, p. 25.)

How do we develop our talents? The following formula can be used:

1. *Discover* talents by examining the strengths and abilities within.
2. *Desire* to put forth the effort to develop the talents.
3. *Faith* in self and Heavenly Father that the task can be accomplished.
4. *Develop* the talents by learning the skills necessary for success.
5. *Mastery* of the skills by continuous effort and practice.
6. *Share* the talents with others so they may benefit from them and see the good works coming from them.

We should pursue excellence to the point where our skills and abilities can be enlarged with greater proficiency to be of service and benefit to others. Here lies the key to our success in life; to be a light unto others which brings joy and happiness in this life and the life to come.

Temporal Law Observance/ Civic Service   19

☐ *Obey the laws of the land; be a loyal patriotic citizen; participate in the improvement of the community and nation.*

"Every Latter-day Saint should sustain, honor, and obey the constitutional law of the land in which he lives" — President Spencer W. Kimball (*Ensign*, May 1974, p. 5).

President Marion G. Romney said: "A Latter-day Saint . . . is not a member of the Church only; he is also a subject or citizen of the state in which he lives. As such, his attitude must be in harmony with the *Twelfth Article of Faith:* 'We believe in being subject to kings, presidents, rulers, and magistrates, in obeying, honoring, and sustaining the law' " (*Ensign,* Jan. 1971, p. 16).

The *Twelfth Article of Faith* is a declaration requiring obedience, loyalty to, and respect for duly constituted laws and the officials administering those laws. Obedience implies a higher attitude than mere submission. Honoring the law is something which is above selfish desires or indulgences. Sustaining the law is to hold up; to keep from falling, that is, to refrain from saying or doing anything which will weaken it or make it ineffective.

Elder Howard W. Hunter has said:

Citizens do not have the right to take the law into their own hands or exercise physical force. The soverign laws of the state must be sustained, and persons living under those laws must obey them for the good of the whole. . . . Laws enacted to promote the welfare of the whole and suppress evil doing are to be strictly obeyed. We must pay tribute to sustain the government in the necessary expense incurred in the protection of life, liberty, property, and in promoting the welfare of all persons (*Improvement Era*, June 1968, pp. 79-80).

Whatever nation we live in, it will be made better and stronger if our own home is strong and good. Our good homes will make good citizens, and good citizens will make our nation a better place in which to live. President Joseph F. Smith said, "The home then is more than a habitation, it is an institution which stands for stability and love in individuals as well as in nations" (*Gospel Doctrine*, p. 300).

"Reverence (is akin) to the respect for law and a contributing factor toward it is reverence for sacred things," President David O. McKay has stated. He further remarked: "Reverence and obedience to law should begin at home. I speak of reverence in connection with obedience to law because a reverent person is law-abiding" (*Conference Report*, Apr. 1937, pp. 30-31).

As citizens of the state, not only are we to obey and uphold the laws of the land, but to safeguard them as well. Patriotism, means to "stand by the country". Each citizen of a nation has the duty to preserve his freedom, that is something that cannot be delegated, for the price of liberty is still eternal vigilance. An ounce of energy in the preservation of freedom is worth a ton of effort to get it back once it is lost.

Are we doing our duty as citizens, to safeguard our freedom and the preservation of the Constitution? Edmund Burke once said: "All that is necessary for the triumph of evil is that good men do nothing." He who has ears to hear and eyes to see can discern by the Spirit and through the words of God's mouthpiece that our liberties are being taken. President Ezra Taft Benson has declared:

> We cannot say that we have not been warned. . . . You and I sustain one man on this earth as God's mouthpiece. We do not need a prophet — we have one; what we desperately need is a listening ear.
>
> Should it be of concern to us when the mouthpiece of the Lord keeps constantly and consistently raising his voice of warning about the loss of our freedom? There are two unrighteous ways to deal with his prophetic words of warning: you can fight them or ignore them. Either course will bring you disaster in the long run. (*God, Family, Country*, p. 383.)

As Latter-day Saints, it is our duty to be faithful. A man cannot be counted among the fully faithful unless he is an active fighter for freedom. Resistance to tyranny is still obedience to God. Many of the prophecies referring to America's preservation are conditional. That is, if we do our duty we can be preserved, and if not, then we shall be destroyed.

The Book of Mormon warns us about being complacent in our thinking that the Lord will protect us no matter what we do. Referring to the devil, it says: "And others will he pacify, and lull them away into carnal security, and they will say: All is well in Zion; yea, Zion prospereth, all is well — and thus the devil cheateth their souls, and leadeth them away *carefully* down to hell." (2 Nephi 28:21, italics added.)

President Ezra Taft Benson has said: "Since God created man with certain inalienable rights, and man, in turn, created government to help secure and safeguard those rights, it follows that man is superior to government and should remain over it, not the other way around. . . . The important thing to keep in mind is that the people who have created their government can give to that government only such powers as they themselves have in the first place." (*God, Family, Country*, p. 284-285.)

As citizens, we form the government by electing (hiring) public officials to work for us in our behalf. Concerning our public officials, the Lord has counseled: "Nevertheless, when the wicked rule the people mourn. Wherefore, honest men and wise men should be sought for diligently, and good men and wise men should observe to uphold; otherwise whatsoever is less than these cometh from evil." (D&C 98:9-10.)

As Latter-day Saints we should pray for our civic leaders and encourage them in righteousness. Our Church leaders have encouraged the saints "to support good and conscientious candidates, of either party, who are aware of the great dangers facing us." (*Deseret News*, Nov. 2, 1964.) We should elect true statesmen that are truly dedicated to the Constitution in the tradition of the founding fathers, and value principles above popularity and work to create popularity for those political principles that are wise and just.

President Ezra Taft Benson has further stated:

> Not only should we seek humble, worthy, courageous leadership; but we should also measure all proposals having to do with our national or local welfare by four standards:
>
> First, is the proposal, the policy, or the idea being promoted, right, as measured by the gospel of Jesus Christ? . . .
>
> Second, is it right as measured by the Lord's standard of constitutional government (see D&C 98:5) . . .
>
> Third, we might well ask, is it right as measured by the counsel of the living oracles of God? It is my conviction that these living oracles are not only authorized,

but are also obligated to give counsel to this people on any subject that is vital to the welfare of this people and to the upbuilding of the kingdom of God. . . .

Fourth, what will be the effect upon the morale and the character of the people if this or that policy is adopted; (*God, Family, Country,* p. 279.)

Our patriotic objectives are for less government, more individual responsibility, and devotion to God. We must be well informed from sources that are consistently accurate on the things of greatest consequence in our lives. Then we must take action as citizens to make it right for the good of all.

How can we "get involved" as citizens in civic affairs? We can register and then vote; assist in campaigning for good and wise candidates for office; lobby for positive and constructive legislation; assist in voter registration at elections, become a volunteer member on civic committees or join service clubs for community improvement; volunteer for moral issue campaigns in defense of gospel principles and standards; or become a committee member for wholesome programs implemented for the good of the community.

If we want a better neighborhood, a better city, state and nation to live in, we must give of our time and energies to see that it happens. We must be devoted to sound principles in word and deed, above party, above pocketbook, and above popularity.

Latter-day Saints have a stewardship — to be a light unto the world for a good cause. May we be as valiant for freedom and righteousness, here and now, as we were when we fought for these principles in the preexistence. We must follow the proverb and eternal truth, "righteousness exalteth a nation", for there is no other safe way.

☐ *Beautify the home and its surroundings; let orderliness reflect a standard unto others; be an example of righteousness in the world.*

"Let your light so shine before men, that they may see your good works and glorify your Father which is in heaven" (Matthew 5:16).

Our earthly possessions — our homes, our lands, our material wealth, even our physical bodies are stewardships given to us in this life by our Father in heaven. As stewards, we are not owners of our material possessions but only manage them for a given time for the Lord, who is the real owner.

We have often heard the statement that "cleanliness is next to Godliness". As Latter-day Saints, we can become a model and a standard for all the people around us by beautifying our homes and surroundings. By doing so, the effort put forth will spawn a feeling of pride and orderliness where the Spirit of the Lord may dwell. Others will catch the same spirit and will foster orderliness and beauty in and around their own surroundings.

President Spencer W. Kimball has said: "The Lord . . . created for us this beautiful world and gave command to our Father Adam to till the ground and to dress the land

and to make it habitable. That command continues to us. We recommend to all people that there be no undue pollution, that the land be taken care of and kept clean, productive, and beautiful" (*Ensign*, May 1975, p. 5).

In Matthew 5:16 it says, "Let your light so shine before men that they may see your good works. . . ." Of this passage, the First Presidency has said: "Our homes and our buildings are showcases of what we believe. They should be attractive and give every indication of cleanliness, orderliness, and self-esteem." (Spencer W. Kimball, N. Eldon Tanner, Marion G. Romney, *Ensign*, May 1976, p. 125.)

Such projects are never ending and need continuous attention and planning. Children should be given responsibilities to help keep the home and surrounding property neat and clean. This involvement by the children will be time far better spent than long hours before the television. It will foster family togetherness and will teach the principles of work and orderliness in living.

* * *

Latter-day Saints also have a stewardship to be an example, a "light unto the world." President Joseph F. Smith spoke of the great blessings that Latter-day Saints have been called to receive: "But all this availeth little or nothing, unless the Saints consider themselves of some consequence, and let their light shine, collectively and individually; unless they are model in their behavior, honest, zealous in the spread of truth, tolerant of their neighbors." (*Gospel Doctrine*, p. 87.)

One fault to be avoided is the tendency for us to live on "borrowed light", with our own light hidden under a bushel and that light within us reflected, rather than original.

We have been called out "of the world" into the kingdom of God, and while we are yet "in the world," we are not of the world in the sense that we are under any necessity to surrender our standards and partake of the false doctrines of the world which are in conflict with the spirit of truth.

President Harold B. Lee has said: "The Church of Jesus Christ of Latter-day Saints stands today as it has always stood, as a continuing revolution against the norms of society that fall below the standards of the Gospel. The failure of the Church to take such a stand would make it unworthy of the sacred name given it by the Lord himself." (*Decisions for Successful Living*, p. 9.)

President Gordon B. Hinckley has given us this counsel with a promise:

> It is not always easy to live in the world and not be a part of it. We cannot live entirely with our own or unto ourselves, nor would we wish to. We must mingle with others. In so doing, we can be gracious. We can be inoffensive. We can avoid any spirit or attitude of self-righteousness. But we can maintain our standards. . . .
>
> Beginning with you and me, there can be an entire people who by the virtue of our lives in our homes, in our vocations, even in our amusements, can become as a city upon a hill to which men may look and learn, and an ensign to the nations from which the people of the earth may gather strength. (*Ensign*, Nov. 1974, p. 100.)

Goal Setting

Setting goals and the decision to reach them are important elements in the success of any endeavor. Once definite goals have been established, specific plans should be made to attain them. The *goal is the target,* and the *plan is the path* taken to reach it. If a worthy goal cannot be attained, a new plan should be adopted, rather than setting a lower goal.

Goals should be:

1. Prayerfully set with guidance from the Spirit.
2. Specific rather than general.
3. Written down.
4. Stated in terms of a specific time period.
5. Set by those responsible for their attainment.
6. Realistic and attainable but should also be challenging.
7. Directed toward helping and serving other people as well as toward self-improvement.
8. Reviewed frequently, and the results reported periodically.

Be honest and soul-searching as goals are selected. Once those goals have been selected, commit to a carefully developed plan to achieve them. Be diligent in following the plan. Account to Heavenly Father regularly concerning progress. It may be helpful to discuss personal goals, plans and progress with an understanding and trusted friend.

Do not undertake at one time more than you can reasonably accomplish. Goals and plans should be challenging but realistic. Wise King Benjamin in the *Book of Mormon* counseled: "And see that all these things are done in wisdom and order; for it is not requisite that a man should run faster than he has strength. And again, it is expedient that he should be diligent, that thereby he might win the prize; therefore, all things must be done in order." (Mosiah 4:27.)

Thus through the principle of "line upon line, precept upon precept; here a little, there a little", growth toward excellence is achieved. (see D&C 128:21.)

Follow the Master's great success formula for bringing to pass the immortality and eternal life of man that Elder Hartman Rector, Jr. outlines: "First, *believe you can do it* . . . Second, *look to the Lord for your blessings* . . . Third, *make the sacrifice* . . . Fourth, *expect the miracle* . . . Fifth, *receive the miracle with great humility.* . . ." (*Ensign*, May 1979, p. 31.)

Planning Guides

The following is an example of a simple approach to recording a goal and a plan to achieve it. Writing the goal and the plan is an important element of success.

WHAT TO DO	HOW TO DO IT	WHEN TO BE DONE
1. Read the Book of Mormon by __(date)__, marking and recording passages of special meaning to me.	1. Obtain an inexpensive copy of the Book of Mormon, colored pencils and a notebook.	1._____ (date)
	2. Develop a system of marking and recording key passages.	2._____ (date)
	3. Read and mark the Book of Mormon at a specific time during the day.	3. From 6:45 a.m. to 7:15 a.m., Mon. through Fri., beginning _____ (date) .
	4. Review the passages marked and record ideas and impressions.	4. Each Sunday, at 2:00 p.m. to 3:00 p.m.
	5. Evaluate progress towards completion of goal.	5. First Sunday of the month.
	6. Record goal, progress and completion in personal journal.	6. Completion date: _____ (date) .

GOAL PLANNING FORM

Keeping my Life in Balance with Worthy Goals.

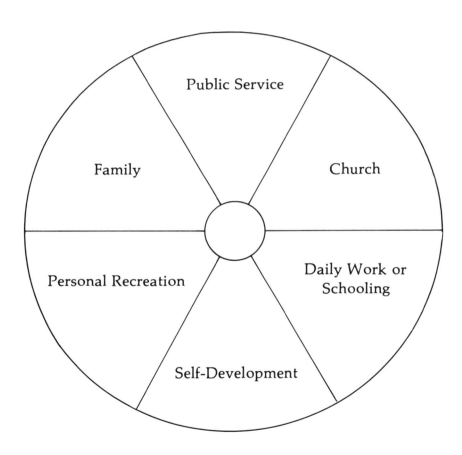